# Repatriation of Indigenous Cultural Heritage

*Repatriation of Indigenous Cultural Heritage* examines how returned materials – objects, photographs, audio, and manuscripts – are being received and reintegrated into the ongoing social and cultural lives of Aboriginal Australians.

Combining a critical examination of the making of these collections with an assessment of their contemporary significance, the book exposes the opportunities and challenges involved in returning cultural heritage for the purposes of maintaining, preserving, or reviving cultural practice. Drawing on ethnographic work undertaken with Aboriginal communities and the institutions that hold significant collections, the author reveals important new insights about the impact of return on communities. Technological advances, combined with the push towards decolonising methodologies in Indigenous research, have resulted in considerable interest in ensuring that collections of cultural value are returned to Indigenous communities. Gibson challenges the rhetoric of museum repatriation, arguing that, while it has been tremendously important to advancing Indigenous interest, it is too often over-simplified.

*Repatriation of Indigenous Cultural Heritage* offers a timely, critical perspective on current museum practice and its place within processes of cultural production and transmission. The book is sure to resonate in other international contexts where questions about Indigenous re-engagement and decolonisation strategies are being debated and will be of interest to students and scholars of Museum Studies, Indigenous Studies, and Anthropology.

**Jason M. Gibson** is Senior Research Fellow and Lecturer in cultural heritage and museum studies at Deakin University, Melbourne, Australia. He has worked extensively with Aboriginal custodians throughout Australia on history, museum, and heritage-related projects and has conducted collaborative ethnographic fieldwork in Central Australia for the past two decades. His first book *Ceremony Men: Making Ethnography and the Return of the Strehlow Collection* (2020) was awarded the Council of Museum Anthropology Book Prize and the Australian Historical Associations' WK Hancock Prize.

**Museums in Focus**
Series Editor
Kylie Message
*Australian National University, Australia*

Committed to the articulation of big, even risky ideas, in small format publications, 'Museums in Focus' challenges authors and readers to experiment with, innovate, and press museums and the intellectual frameworks through which we view these. It offers a platform for approaches that radically rethink the relationships between cultural and intellectual dissent and crisis and debates about museums, politics and the broader public sphere.

'Museums in Focus' is motivated by the intellectual hypothesis that museums are not innately 'useful', safe' or even 'public' places, and that recalibrating our thinking about them might benefit from adopting a more radical and oppositional form of logic and approach. Examining this problem requires a level of comfort with (or at least tolerance of) the idea of crisis, dissent, protest and radical thinking, and authors might benefit from considering how cultural and intellectual crisis, regeneration and anxiety have been dealt with in other disciplines and contexts.

The following list includes only the most-recent titles to publish within the series. A list of the full catalogue of titles is available at: www.routledge.com/Museums-in-Focus/book-series/MIF

**Reflections on Critical Museology**
Inside and Outside Museums
*J. Pedro Lorente*

**Self-Determined First Nations Museums and Colonial Contestation**
The Keeping Place
*Robert Hudson and Shannon Woodcock*

**Repatriation of Indigenous Cultural Heritage**
Experiences of Return in Central Australia
*Jason M. Gibson*

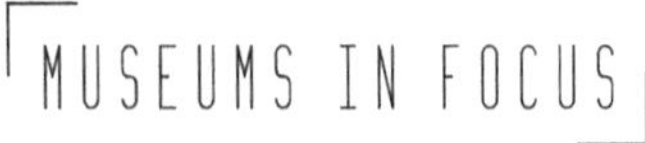


Logo by James Verdon (2017)

# Repatriation of Indigenous Cultural Heritage

## Experiences of Return in Central Australia

**Jason M. Gibson**

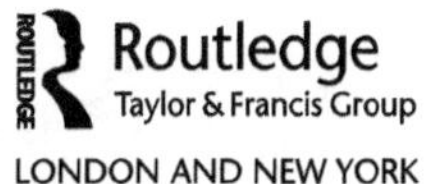


LONDON AND NEW YORK

First published 2024
by Routledge
4 Park Square, Milton Park, Abingdon, Oxon OX14 4RN

and by Routledge
605 Third Avenue, New York, NY 10158

*Routledge is an imprint of the Taylor & Francis Group, an informa business*



*British Library Cataloguing-in-Publication Data*
A catalogue record for this book is available from the British Library

*Library of Congress Cataloging-in-Publication Data*
Names: Gibson, Jason M. (Jason Matthew), 1976– author.
Title: Repatriation of indigenous cultural heritage : experiences of return in central Australia / Jason M. Gibson.
Other titles: Experiences of return in central Australia
Description: Abingdon, Oxon ; New York, NY : Routledge, 2024. | Series: Museums in focus | Includes bibliographical references and index. | Contents: Re-engagements with Indigenous Collections after the Return — Indigenous Appropriations of Anthropological Photography and Collections Putting Objects Back in Place — Digital Returns of Anmatyerr Ceremonial Performance and New Collecting Transformative Collaborations in Australian Ethnographic Collections Reflections on Return.
Identifiers: LCCN 2023011827 (print) | LCCN 2023011828 (ebook) | ISBN 9780367745097 (hbk) | ISBN 9780367746230 (pbk) | ISBN 9781003158752 (ebk)
Subjects: LCSH: Aboriginal Australians—Material culture. | Cultural property—Repatriation—Australia. | Ethnological museums and collections—Australia.
Classification: LCC DU124.M37 G53 2024 (print) | LCC DU124.M37 (ebook) | DDC 363.6/90899915094—dc23/eng/20230403
LC record available at https://lccn.loc.gov/2023011827
LC ebook record available at https://lccn.loc.gov/2023011828

ISBN: 978-0-367-74509-7 (hbk)
ISBN: 978-0-367-74623-0 (pbk)
ISBN: 978-1-003-15875-2 (ebk)

DOI: 10.4324/9781003158752

Typeset in Times New Roman
by Apex CoVantage, LLC

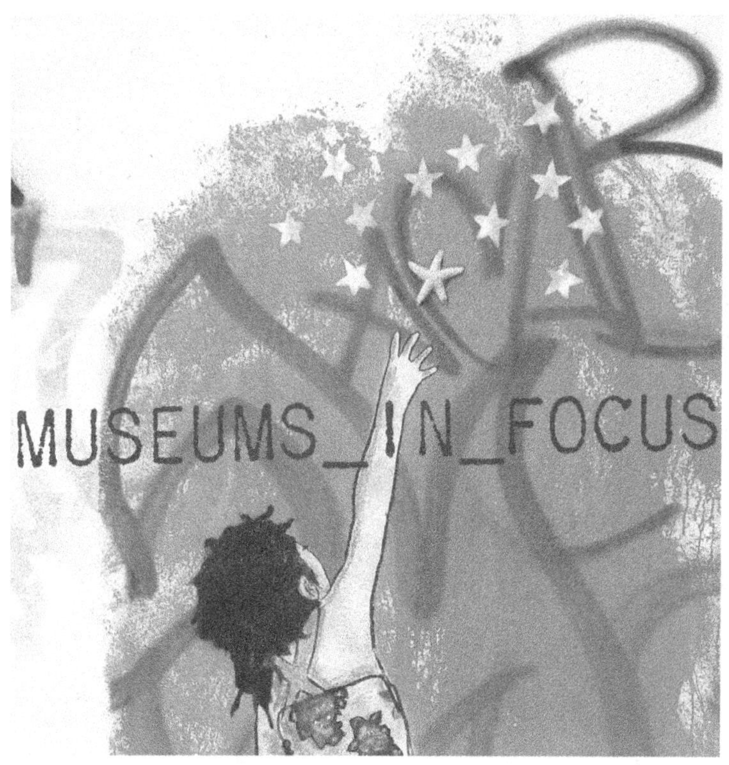


**Anonymous graffiti, Athens. Image and logo by James Verdon (2017).**

# Contents


| | | |
|---|---|---|
| | *List of Figures* | *viii* |
| | *Acknowledgements* | *ix* |
| 1 | Introduction: Re-engagements with Indigenous Collections After the Return | 1 |
| 2 | Indigenous Appropriations of Anthropological Photography and Collections | 16 |
| 3 | Putting Objects Back in Place | 36 |
| 4 | Digital Returns of Anmatyerr Ceremonial Performance and New Collecting | 54 |
| 5 | Transformative Collaborations in Australian Ethnographic Collections | 71 |
| 6 | Conclusion: Reflections on Return | 92 |
| | *Index* | *106* |

# Figures

2.1 Going over Tommy Thompson's photographic collection with him in 2017 19
2.2 The male Arrernte emoji and Spencer's photograph of an unnamed Arrernte man 21
2.3 The female Arrernte emoji and Gillen's photograph of an unnamed Arrernte woman 21
2.4 Joel Liddle with his artwork depicting Arrernte elder Irrapmwe Peltharre overlaying sketch drawing of the colonial explorer John McDouall Stuart 25
2.5 Joseph Yugi Williams at the Melbourne Museum in 2022 28
2.6 Painted shield attributed to Tracker Nat Williams depicting Warumungu hunter approaching a red kangaroo and an emu 31
4.1 Anmatyerr men Martin Hagan (R) and Michael Tommy (L) painting ceremonial shields for their archive at Laramba 65

# Acknowledgements

The research outlined in this book was carried out over many years and was made possible by a Discovery Early Career Researcher Award from the Australian Research Council (DE220100206). Considerable support was also provided by the Alfred Deakin Institute for Citizenship and Globalisation at Deakin University (Melbourne) and its various postdoctoral fellowship schemes. The ideas have been developed in discussion with numerous colleagues at Deakin University, including Andrea Witcomb, Gaye Sculthorpe, Virginie Rey, Billy Griffiths, Helen Gardner, Melinda Hinkson, Luke Scholes, Michael Cawthorn, and Tiffany Shellam. Beyond Deakin, I would also like to thank the following for either reading drafts or engaging conversations that shaped my thinking: Alistair Paterson, Vanessa Russ, Shaun Angeles, John Carty, Darren Jorgensen, Catherine Bishop, Levi McLean, John Kean, Phillip Batty, Michael Aird, Jilda Andrews, Iain Johnston, Chris Anderson, Michael Pickering, Myfany Turpin, Jennifer Green, Aaron Glass, and Fred Myers. I would particularly like to thank Howard Morphy for suggesting this book for the *Museums in Focus Series*, editor Kylie Message for her willingness to test the idea, and Heidi Lowther at Routledge. Andrew Stapleton at the Alfred Deakin Institute provided excellent editorial feedback.

It will be obvious to readers of the book that I owe an enormous debt to numerous Aboriginal people from across Australia but, in particular, to Anmatyerr and Arrernte people who have hosted me in their communities for close to two decades. My main teachers in this domain have been elders such as Paddy Willis, Eric Penangk, Huckitta Lynch, Max Tilmouth, Peter Satfford, Michael Tommy, Ronnie McNamara, Ken Tilmouth, Jimmy Haines, and Tony Scrutton. A significant group of younger people has also come to the fore in terms of their passion and interest in the museum and archival collections. In the Arandic region, men such as Shaun Angeles, Joel Liddle, Martin Hagan, Franky Gorey, Wayne Scrutton, and Michael Liddle have generously shared their ideas with me, and elsewhere in the Australian deserts, Joseph 'Yugi' Williams (Warumungu), Jamie Hampton (Warlpiri), Robert McKay (Jaru), and Winston Green (Ngaanyatjarra) have been equally charitable. Beyond Central Australia, I would like to thank members of the Kurnai and

Yuin communities in southeastern Australia, who have taught me about their cultural heritage and history in recent years. Warren Foster and Dan Morgan were very generous in their Yuin country during various trips in 2020 and 2021, and Russell Mullet was a hugely important Kurnai collaborator in Gippsland between 2017 and 2019. Several cultural institutions have also provided important research assistance, including the Melbourne Museum, the National Museum of Australia, the South Australian Museum, the Strehlow Research Centre, and the Berndt Museum of Anthropology.

Enormous thanks to Ada and Arthur, as always, for being everything.

# 1 Introduction

## Re-engagements with Indigenous Collections After the Return

This book stems from more than two decades of engagement with the collecting sector and Aboriginal communities in Australia. As a student in the late 1990s, I was fortunate enough to have the opportunity to talk with Arabana and Adnyamathanha peoples in northern South Australia about their visions for the newly emergent digital society. While some people signalled anxieties about the dissemination of culturally sensitive information, the overwhelming vision was to find ways of bolstering local stories and Aboriginal perspectives. In particular, people wanted to find ways to tell their own stories, reveal their own histories, and have greater access to, and control over, cultural collections (including photographic collections, artworks, sound recordings, and artefacts) pertinent to them. Soon after, numerous projects designed to deliver digital information and cultural heritage services to remote Aboriginal communities were underway. I was lucky enough to work for Aboriginal community groups, as well as libraries and museums, on projects that saw significant cultural and historical materials return to their communities of origin. As a museum professional and researcher, I also assisted with repatriation initiatives and developed other ways of linking Aboriginal communities with their key ethnographic collections.

*Repatriation of Indigenous Cultural Heritage* draws from these varied involvements to unpack key ideas that are often taken for granted by the collecting sector and academia but also within the source communities themselves. This book presents entirely new research based on detailed knowledge of the processes involved in return and re-engagement from across a number of Aboriginal communities. Having previously written on the history of anthropological collections (Gibson 2020, 2019) and processes of digital repatriation in Central Australia (Gibson 2021; Gibson & Batty 2014), this book takes a wider scope (encompassing research with Aboriginal communities in both remote and regional Australia) and presents a novel articulation of the impacts of returned collections. Over four chapters, this book interrogates the rhetoric of repatriation, proposes models, and methods for collaborative collections analysis and reveals the joys and insights, as well as the anxieties and complexities, which return can produce. It is important to point out,

DOI: 10.4324/9781003158752-1

however, that I have deliberately excluded the discussion of the repatriation of human remains. I have done this because the topic has been covered very well elsewhere (Fforde, McKeown & Keeler 2020; Kakaliouras 2012; Turnbull & Pickering 2010; Wergin 2021) but also because my own experiences have been exclusively grounded in the return of cultural collections (material culture, audio–visual materials, and textual). Each chapter, therefore, provides descriptions of cultural collections being returned to Aboriginal communities and investigates varied effects on (1) conceptions of place, (2) personhood and cultural identity, (3) cultural revival and education, and (4) postcolonial relations. Although the examples presented here are primarily drawn from Aboriginal Australia (particularly Central Australia), and distinctive ontological and epistemological considerations are critical (Morphy 1992; Myers 2002), key debates, conceptual issues, and challenges will be familiar to other social settings. Each of the chapters highlights the role of individuals and small collectivities in various communities as they strive to access, understand, and reintegrate cultural and historical collections back into their personal and collective lives. As the methodology is primarily ethnographic, focusing on the informal, intersubjective, and everyday experiences of the museum and archival return, the aim is to spark critical dialogue about the interwoven relationships of collection institutions, individuals, and groups.

The themes of this book are most likely to resonate in several settler-colonial states, such as Australia, New Zealand, Canada, and the United States. Although Australian-centric, the themes of the book are also likely to resonate in other international contexts where questions about Indigenous re-engagement and decolonisation strategies are being debated. In settler colonies such as Australia, however, a long history of Indigenous museum activism has led to reasonably well-funded repatriation programmes and various Indigenous access initiatives (Ames 1988; Nash & Colwell-Chanthaphonh 2010; Pickering 2010). The interrogation of cultural collections is now part of a larger critical examination of colonial legacies in these nations, and there is growing acknowledgement of Indigenous people's present-day connection to museum and archive collections as tools for furthering their own knowledge of culture and ensuring the rights of access. While not all collecting institutions agree on the methods and policies, the principle of greater Indigenous engagement with collections has achieved considerable sway. However, what happens when collection materials re-enter the mutable social worlds of their source communities, intermingle with local epistemologies and ontologies, and re-circulate among groups is less well known. The moral and political imperatives of Indigenous stewardship and repatriation have tended to surpass research into what happens 'after the return'.

It was at the opening of a conference at the Alice Springs Convention Centre in 2013 that I began to reflect upon my own role in these processes. As the crowd of mostly non-Indigenous professionals gathered, we were informed that a group of young Arrernte men were about to perform a 'special welcoming dance' that had not been performed for over a century. Having spent the previous three years working on the development of a website that brought together the collections of anthropologists Walter Baldwin Spencer and Francis Gillen (see Chapter 2), much of which featured the Arrernte people, I was naturally curious to see the event. Jockeying for a good position close to the performance space, I was startled to hear the presenter announce that the dance had been re-learnt via the Spencer and Gillen website. Although our project team had consulted widely with Arrernte people about the making of this site, we had not worked directly with these particular people. News of the website had apparently spread quickly, and some of the contents had been taken up in support of cultural revival. After introducing the re-enactment, the two Arrernte leaders (Rosalie Riley and Frank Ansell) proceeded to explain to the crowd how fortunate they were to have Spencer and Gillen's collections to draw upon.

In addition to my interest in how readily (and rapidly) Spencer's film had been utilised by the community, I also thought it notable that the community had expressed such gratitude to past collectors. The general trend among Aboriginal activists and museum professionals in recent years had been to downplay the significance of collectors, and Spencer, in particular, had been widely condemned for his social evolutionism. For these Arrernte people, however, Spencer and Gillen's ethnography was regarded as enormously useful, as it could be meaningfully repurposed to celebrate and revive the cultural practice.

Even though I had been an employee, consultant, and researcher affiliated with different collecting institutions for well over a decade, serendipitously coming across the results of this return began the initial thinking for this book. My motivations have always been to assist Indigenous communities to 'speak back' to the powers of colonialism and proffer a critique of Western ontologies and epistemologies. I continue to accept that museums have often operated as handmaidens to colonialism, and their collections have been used to promulgate certain ideas about what, and who, Indigenous peoples are (Bennett et al. 2017). Yet, after years of poring over collection documentation, meeting with different Aboriginal communities, and investigating the histories of some of Australia's most significant ethnographic collections, I have come to realise the multiple agencies and interests invested in these assemblages provide an opportunity for retracing cultural trajectories. As collections are rarely simple entities, they can carry complex histories of Indigenous and non-Indigenous interaction, contain deep cultural knowledge, and can spur the full range of responses from contemporary generations. As the examples in this book illustrate, returned objects can spark great controversy, produce disquiet, or even be ignored, but they can also become key motivators for cultural edification.

## After the Return

Rather than attempting to add to the already extensive literature on the repatriation debate and Indigenous rights to cultural heritage, this book takes a slightly different tack. Contributing to a much smaller, yet growing body of research concerned with what happens after materials are returned, this book seeks to understand how communities deal with increased access to cultural heritage at the local level. What happens after the museum hands over objects, copies of audio–visual material, digital manuscripts, and transcripts (see Chapter 4)? It is imperative to reflect upon how this might affect communities, but also how this new paradigm transforms museum practices, processes, and policies (see Chapter 5). As the following anecdote demonstrates, Aboriginal communities not only argue for and expect museums to provide enhanced access to and control over their collections but also want museums to recognise that they ought to be accountable to their source communities. As is demonstrated here (particularly in Chapter 4), this accountability extends well beyond the return itself.

In 2012, the highly regarded Yolngu elder Joe Gumbula visited the Melbourne Museum to inspect collections of relevance to his clan and family. This was not the first time Gumbula had visited the museum, and he had been part of various Yolngu delegations to cultural institutions across the globe arguing for the return of ancestral remains and digital repatriation. At the conclusion of this particular visit though, he pondered the legacy of his work and how it would be remembered. He had spent a number of days in the museum, inspecting collections, recommending conservation treatments for different objects, and advising on cultural significance and context. Turning to Lindy Allen, the curator for Northern Australian Indigenous Collections, he asked how his grandchildren would know that he had been to the museum. How would they access the information and knowledge that he had shared with Lindy and the other museum staff? Would there be a record of his visit? How would it be recorded? How could he ensure that future generations could access his commentary and advice to the museum? His questioning not only signalled an acceptance that museums would continue to care for Yolngu cultural materials into the future but also served as a reminder to museums that they needed to better elevate Indigenous perspectives and consider their obligations to source communities in the long term.[1]

Notwithstanding the continuing and significant obstacles to improved Indigenous engagement with collections, there is, nevertheless, a growing institutional acknowledgement that Indigenous cultural heritage deserves to be returned to relevant communities in some way. What happens once these materials arrive in a community and how they are circulated, debated, discussed,

1 Personal Communication with Lindy Allen 01/09/2020.

used, and re-integrated have been less of a concern for these institutions that tend to walk away once their obligation to return has been fulfilled. But how do communities receive and re-integrate these objects and their associated knowledge? Are community responses and critiques of the collection ever recorded or allowed to speak back to the archive? Does their response help shape and influence collecting policies, curation, and collection management? While attempting to answer these questions, I have come to think about the last few decades as ushering in a new era in collecting institutions and Indigenous community relations. The long-term activism of Indigenous peoples, the ubiquity of digitisation and digital networks, postcolonial theory, and the rise of decolonisation narratives have converged to create the current milieu in museum studies and anthropology. If this trend is to continue, which I believe it will, it is important for scholars of the humanities and social sciences to develop a better understanding of the historical context in which these materials were gathered and to re-think their significance in the present. We need to ask what they mean for different communities today. What actions do they make possible, and how might we creatively explore their latent possibilities?

This is a growing area of study and there have already been some excellent analyses documenting the lead up to, and initial responses to, repatriation (Turnbull & Pickering 2010; Tythacott & Arvanitis 2014; Bell, Christen & Turin 2013). This book, therefore, builds upon significant studies on the processes of repatriation as a 'ritual' (Batty 2005; Peers, Reinius & Shannon 2017), the relationship between museum and source community (Brown & Peers 2003; Golding & Modest 2013), and methods of 'archival return' (Barwick, Green & Vaarzon-Morel 2019). I tackle the question of what happens after the return through a series of case studies that demonstrate how collections – which I define as encompassing museum, library, and archive collections – circulate through social networks, inform relationships to place, and play a role in the constitution of cultural selves and collectivities. As objects move from lifeless institutional spaces into the social fields of a community, collections become animated and begin to generate new relationships among and between people. The intention of the book then is to illustrate these generative qualities of museum collections as they produce both positive social impacts and introduce new challenges. Understanding these processes has not traditionally been a primary concern for museums. Museum staff works diligently to identify object provenance, they employ protocols to manage materials, and they will consult with source communities but rarely will they interrogate the mid- to long-term effects of repatriation and return. Primarily concerned with an object's existence within its four walls, the museum ultimately trusts that source communities will have the wherewithal to care for their cultural heritage once it is given back. In fact, museums have, for good reasons, tended to maintain a distance from the intensely local/personal concerns for fear of becoming too deeply embroiled in matters exterior to their institutional purview.

Achieving a better understanding of how collections are being utilised, debated, re-interpreted, and cared for outside of the institution is, therefore, best accomplished via collaborative ethnographic research. The ethnographic research presented in these chapters advances this objective by presenting varied experiences and reflections of working with Aboriginal communities as they access, interpret, and utilise collections with the objective of mediating returned cultural knowledge. Understanding the lifeworlds into which collections return – where ideas and passions, moral norms, and ethical dilemmas play out – may result in better-informed museum policy and practice. There are only a small number of published ethnographies of repatriation (Bolton 2015) although this research is likely to grow in the coming years. My use of the concept of the 'lifeworld', rather than the more commonly used terms, such as 'culture' or 'society', is a deliberate one aimed at accentuating the animated, variable, and vital social fields that people operate within (Jackson 2013, p. 7). The notion permits a greater permeability when thinking about relationships, resists reliance upon the bounded conception of social and cultural identities (in particular Indigenous and non-Indigenous), and encourages closer analyses of moments of exchange. This is critical if we wish to better understand the various agencies at play when objects re-enter community life.

## Object Trajectories

Keywords such as *repatriation, recuperation, renewal, restoration, rediscovery,* and *revival* feature heavily in research relating to Indigenous access to museum collections. Each word shares the Latin prefix *re-*, meaning 'again' or 'again and again', and tends to signify the general trajectory of cultural objects as they move in and out of cultural, institutional, or geographical boundaries. While this movement is generally presented as a unidirectional transaction, whereby cultural objects are presumably liberated from collection stores and sent back to their rightful recipients, the reality is often far more complex. Conceiving these transactions in this way overlooks the often-complicated histories that communities have had with different collectors in the past and their current concerns about some objects returning, especially where capacities to make confident decisions about custodianship/ownership are strained. The examples discussed in this book illustrate how objects do not necessarily move along linear trajectories back to their communities but are staying in museums, being loaned, interrogated, and/or copied and disseminated.

As more and more communities lobby for access, enter museums, and engage with the histories of their collections, the trajectories of these objects – through time and place – come into view. A shield that is now discussed as having been collected by the Cook expedition at Botany Bay in 1770, for example, has lived many lives (Nugent & Sculthorpe 2018). Although research into the object's provenance and biography is inconclusive, since the 1960s, it has been generally thought of as a likely survival from the 'first contact' between Australian Aboriginal people and the first British colonial voyagers. The shield seems to have arrived at the British Museum via the private collection of Joseph Banks c.1817, formally registered into the collection in 1978, and selected for display in the Enlightenment Gallery in 2003. In 2015, the so-called 'Cook shield' was selected as a 'pivotal' exhibit in the *Indigenous Australia: Enduring Civilization* exhibition in London and subsequently activated repatriation claims from descendants of the Gweagal people of Kamay (Botany Bay). Now publicly discussed as 'the Gweagal shield', the demands of some Aboriginal people for the object to be repatriated have led some to argue for 'basic colonial reparations' (Keenan 2017) regardless of the apparent tensions over ownership and rights that exist between different Aboriginal stakeholder groups (Timbery 2020). The repatriation claim has to date been unsuccessful, largely due to the questionable interpretative leaps made by some of the claimants and the differences of opinion within the Aboriginal community about the object's future. These engagements have nonetheless generated new historical knowledge about the shield via intensive scholarship (Thomas 2018), produced incredibly positive collaborations between the relevant communities and museum professionals and academics, and stimulated the emergence of new Indigenous-led research and artistic practice.

There is a growing number of communities now knocking on the doors of museums, speaking assertively about their cultural heritage, and demanding a say in its management. The interventions of the Haida peoples of British Columbia (Canada) at the Pitt River Museum, for example, led to careful reflection on the need to cultivate and sustain reciprocity between communities and institutions (Krmpotich & Peers 2013). This marks yet another stage in the history of collections. The *repatriation* or *return* of cultural heritage objects (distinctions that I discuss later) and the part they might play in the *restoration* or *renewal* of histories, cultural knowledge, and practices ought not, therefore, be considered the endpoint of this process but part of the continuing passage of things and ideas across time and space. As illustrated in the various examples discussed throughout this book, attempts to return Indigenous content to communities rarely result in a complete disengagement from larger institutional, social, and historical connections. It is for this reason that I have adopted Paul Basu's notion of *re-entanglement* as a far more accurate description of what occurs when communities are refamiliarised with collections. Basu extends Thomas's highly influential idea that ethnographic objects are inherently 'entangled' in processes of mutual appropriation and unequal exchange on the colonial frontier and argues that these complexities are accessed anew as they become *re-entangled* in the present. Returning the collections of the colonial anthropologist Northcote W. Thomas to communities in Nigeria and Sierra Leone, Basu has shown how these communities willingly re-entangled themselves in these difficult colonial histories in the hope of uncovering latent potentialities in the material.[2]

Rather than simply accepting the museum and archival collections as instruments of colonial domination or tainted by colonial forms and logics of knowledge (Dirks 1993, p. 310), re-entanglement describes a form of collections activism. It permits a reappraisal of what the 'decolonial affordances' of these ethnographic collections might be for a range of stakeholders (Basu & Jong 2016) and asks how these materials might be appropriated. While the more conventional notion of repatriation has been tremendously important for advancing Indigenous interests and rights in collections, it does not adequately capture the range of affordances that collections offer. In Australia, for example, demands for the physical repatriation of objects have been minimal despite the publicity that these claims generate. Museums and communities everywhere are experimenting with other measures aimed at improving community collaborations, such as the establishment of long-term loans, co-curation, co-conservation, and developing new online access platforms (Kreps 2009; Silverman 2015; Hamilton 2017; Morphy 2020). As a conceptual tool, the rhetoric of repatriation helps us understand the significance of physically returning objects to ameliorate colonial legacies (especially where they have been illicitly removed); however, it offers limited scope for considering where collection objects go, how they might be reconnected to their cultures of origin, and understanding the plethora of ways that they might be managed and utilised by communities into the future. It is for these reasons that I use the term 'return' rather than 'repatriation' throughout the book.

Projects to return to and conduct community-led interrogations of ethnographic collections are at the forefront of contemporary museum practice. Recent exhibitions and digital initiatives that connected the collections of the seminal anthropologist Franz Boas are a case in point. Developed by the Bard Graduate Center in partnership with the U'mista Cultural Centre of Alert Bay in British Columbia, the *Story Box* exhibition provides the Kwakwa̱ka̱'wakw community an opportunity to 'reactivate' the collection through object reproductions, critical annotations of Boas's anthropological texts, and their reflections on Boas's Tlingit informant and collaborator, George Hunt.[3] In projects like this, the history of an object or collection will travel with it, but its material form, mode of circulation, and interpretation will often be entirely novel.

## Ethnographic Collections

The collections discussed in this book were principally collected by anthropologists of the late nineteenth and early twentieth centuries. As noted earlier,

2 Personal Communication via email with Paul Basu 23/10/2019.

3 http://exhibitions.bgc.bard.edu/storybox/.

I first came to learn about these collections while working with Aboriginal communities in Central and Northern Australia at a time when the establishment of local, digital archives was on the rise. I began approaching various collecting institutions across Australia asking for information about any collection items – mainly photographic or audio–visual – that could be digitised and copied for local, community access. I would also join community members on trips to capital city museums where we would reconnoiter storerooms, ask probing questions of curators about collection histories, and negotiate ways of gaining better access to selected items. These experiences led to my professional employment on various research projects concerning some of Australia's most important ethnographic collections, including the early work of A. W. Howitt and Lorimer Fison (1872–1904), their successors Walter Baldwin Spencer and Francis Gillen (1894–1927), the linguist/ethnographer Theodor George Heinrich (T. G. H.) Strehlow (1932–1971), and the anthropological duo of Ronald and Catherine Berndt (1939–1986).

As a non-Indigenous anthropologist working with communities as they come to these collections (sometimes for the first time), I have been privileged to have shared in some of the pleasures of 'return'. I have been present when expert singers have sung over the top of song recordings more than a century old; I have been able to reconnect people to objects collected from their grandfathers; and I have been lucky enough to share in the excited conversations that occur outside of the museum following a successful community visit. Entering into dialogue with people about the inherent power of objects, the sentience and eternal character of the place and the presence of Ancestors in (and out of) museum stores have admittedly tested my capacities as a researcher (see Chapter 3). I cannot claim this knowledge as my own, but, as an attentive witness and participant, I accept this testimony and attempt to exist in relation to it respectfully. These tenets of reflexive ethnography have opened me up to an appreciation of some of the issues that people face when items of cultural significance, or materials imbued with potent cultural knowledge, return.

However, finding ways of utilising collections that were originally produced during times when anthropological enquiry concerned itself with either salvaging or ordering the world of 'Others' presents significant challenges. The colonial foundations of museums carried a thinly veiled Eurocentrism and a commitment to scientific endeavour and evolutionism that informed forms of colonial governance. Ethnographic collecting and its related exhibitionary practices, therefore, helped promulgate the idea of hierarchical developmental sequences in human development and negatively impacted upon perceptions of Indigenous peoples (Russell 2001; Bennett et al. 2017). This was, however, not always the case. The discipline of anthropology had, from its early stages, contained an anti-colonial orientation through its promotion of greater historical particularism, its desire to better understand and appreciate the cultural difference, and its commitment to documentation (Morphy

2020, pp. 107–108). Many of the discipline's most important figures, which ethnomusicologist Michael Asch argues, would now be 'overjoyed' to learn that the very cultures that they recorded 'in fear of their demise are still here (notwithstanding colonialism)' (2015, p. 486). Furthermore, they would likely be pleased to learn that their texts and collections were being used for cultural education and revival.

Decades of activism by Indigenous groups in settler-colonial societies, combined with the influences of postcolonialism and decolonisation across the social sciences and humanities (Smith 1999; Tuck & Yang 2012; Turner 2015; Onciul 2015), have had a tremendous impact on the way ethnographic collections are being re-considered. The significant social and political changes of the 1960s and 1970s have radically changed relations between Indigenous and non-Indigenous peoples. The various Indigenous rights movements in post-settler-colonial nations and the emergence of new social policies effectively ended the way self-appointed non-Indigenous peoples, and institutions such as museums could simply assume proprietorship over all things Indigenous. This new sociopolitical context, combined with anthropology's pre-existing interest in cultural differences, meant that anthropologists working with ethnographic collections were often the first within these museums to embrace inclusive and collaborative practices. As (Thomas 2019) writes, these people:

> recognised responsibilities to engage with the descendants of people who had made the artefacts from which collections were made. Consultative practice developed in fits and starts and the concept of the museum as a space of cross-cultural engagement and encounter became fundamental, and was subsequently embraced by the whole museum sector, from history and science to art institutions: it is now widely affirmed that the museum should be a meeting place, a realm of diversity and dialogue.

The interface between Aboriginal communities and collecting institutions, where dialogue and action around repatriation and reconnection with cultural heritage occur, is arguably one of the most important to the future of museums. This complex field of negotiation, often intermixed with bureaucratic processes, ideological agendas, and community politics, is now one of the most important domains for those working with ethnographic collections. What was once a vocation concerned with the elaboration of object typologies and analyses of humanity's development is now increasingly focused on the interests of living cultures and communities.

People will, therefore, often approach these collections with the expectation that they possess 'Indigenous knowledge'. While an incredibly important and growing body of work has unveiled the key roles that Indigenous peoples played in early collecting (Konishi, Nugent & Shellam 2015), their agency in the making of collections (Gibson 2020), and their brokerage in forming exhibitions' displays (Glass 2006), the 'knowledge' found in ethnographic collections is rarely ever wholly 'Indigenous'. While ethnographic collections do certainly possess important insights into Indigenous worldviews, practices, and customs, there are important epistemological questions that need to be considered. Knowledge is not a discrete, bounded parcel of information transferable via objects but something mutually constituted through dialogue between the collector and collected, the scribe, and the cultural expert. As such, it will also often involve misinterpretation and misunderstanding as much as interpretation and understanding. Ethnographic objects are, as Barbara Kirshenblatt-Gimblett (1998, p. 2) argues, equally 'objects of ethnography', as they also tell us a great deal about the Western discipline/s that gave rise to them. Moreover, our own contemporary reading and framing of these texts and objects will additionally affect the type of knowledge that we ascertain for them.

## Reverse Fieldwork

Delving into collections with these types of questions in mind requires a methodology fit for the purpose. There is a need to move beyond analyses of a collection's history and its making and into the arguably more demanding work of reconnecting (sometimes patchily documented) collections with present-day people and communities. Scholarship concerning collaborations between museums, curators, and communities has revealed just how important it is for platforms of 'shared authority' to be established when developing research, publications, and exhibitions (Hutchison 2013). Writing about contemporary Native American engagements with museum objects across multiple institutions, Abenaki scholar, Margaret Bruchac, provides one of the best descriptions of a useful methodology. Described as 'reverse ethnography' or 'reverse fieldwork', Bruchac argues for a process, whereby communities are enabled to 'cross-walk' through archives and collections and 'to track objects and their related stories (even the false or fishy stories) through the locales and tribal nations represented in collections' (2018, p. 183). The aim is to generate new knowledge by questioning the supposed authority of museum catalogue entries and support people in ways that allow them to discuss, research, and ponder expansive object relationships (not just between objects, but with people, places, and stories).

It is important that 'reverse fieldwork' can occur across different collections and institutions. However, the logistical challenges of linking data in disparate catalogues, interrogating museum documentation, and dealing with disconnections and misinterpretations between collections ought not to be downplayed. However, being able to retrospectively examine moments of collection and acquisition and, moreover, map the cartography of object circulation, as Bruchac argues, is critical to restoring connections with present-day lives. As illustrated in this short book, Aboriginal research into collections of ceremonial objects has been significantly aided by the sharing of collections data from multiple institutions with communities that are then able to make sense of the linkages using their highly specialised cultural expertise. While some sceptical curators may contest the idea that these people might hold useful information relevant to historic objects, examples in this book show how input from source communities can resolve mysteries surrounding object provenance and/or provide further information on an item's historical and contemporary meaning. Opening up data and sharing ideas, while, at the same time, allowing Indigenous groups the ability to set their own limits to this circulation, can lead to significant outcomes for all.

A crucial aspect of museum work, including these types of flexible and collaborative investigations, is the basic object and collection research. Close archival and collection-based research, although criticised as referencing the 'enlightenment' traditions of empiricism and connoisseurship and, thus, working against efforts to decolonise imperial and colonial institutions, remains critical. The experienced and highly respected Aboriginal curator Shaun Angeles, for example, has spoken powerfully about the need for museums to carefully and accurately research and document their collections (Gibson, Angeles & Liddle 2019, p. 43). Speaking about the Canadian context, Ruth Phillips similarly reminds us that basic research is still at a very preliminary stage for the majority of Native North American museum objects, and questions of style, periodisation, and historical context go beyond the purely academic. These can, in fact, be 'urgent' questions for:

> movements of cultural renewal and claims for the repatriation of museum objects, both of which depend on the ability to establish local histories of production, use, and exchange. . . . In this sense, collection-based research and the sharing of its results with originating communities is itself a form of repatriation.
>
> (Phillips 2005, p. 94)

What needs to change is the style of consultation that has traditionally occurred in the repatriation context. As an Indigenous scholar interested in teasing out the histories and meanings of collections for present and future generations, Bruchac's work on Native American archaeological and anthropological materials has shown that museums need to go beyond the standard formalised types of 'consultation' around repatriation. She notes that these consultations usually focus upon one object, or a small collection of objects, and are generally concerned with questions of ownership, which subsequently tends to become mired in 'legal matters' and 'positional power'. Replacing these 'consultations' with more 'open-ended conversations' that encourage relaxed social interaction and freedom to share memories and insights would, in Bruchac's estimation, be far more fruitful (2018, p. 184).

I hope that the experiences contained within this book come close to this open-ended, conversational model. If museum anthropology has a future, then, surely, it will be grounded in a restorative approach to relationships between people, objects, collecting institutions, and communities.

## References

Ames, M.M. 1988, 'Proposals for Improving Relations between Museums and the Indigenous Peoples of Canada', *Museum Anthropology*, vol. 12, no. 3, pp. 15–19.

Asch, M. 2015, 'Anthropology, Colonialism and the Reflexive Turn: Finding a Place to Stand', *Anthropologica*, vol. 57, no. 2, pp. 481–489.

Barwick, L., Green, J.A. & Vaarzon-Morel, P. (eds). 2019, *Archival Returns: Central Australia and Beyond*, University of Hawaii Press, Honolulu.

Basu, P. & Jong, F.D. 2016, 'Utopian Archives, Decolonial Affordances Introduction to Special Issue', *Social Anthropology*, vol. 24, no. 1, pp. 5–19.

Batty, P. 2005, 'White Redemption Rituals: Repatriating Aboriginal Secret-Sacred Objects', *Arena Journal*, no. 23, p. 29.

Bell, J.A., Christen, K. & Turin, M. 2013, 'Introduction: After the Return', *Museum Anthropology Review*, vol. 7, no. 1–2, pp. 1–21.

Bennett, T., Cameron, F., Dias, N., Dibley, B., Harrison, R., Jacknis, I. & McCarthy, C. 2017, *Collecting, Ordering, Governing: Anthropology, Museums, and Liberal Government*, Duke University Press, Durham.

Bolton, L. 2015, 'An Ethnography of Repatriation: Engagements with Erromango, Vanuatu', in *The International Handbooks of Museum Studies*, John Wiley & Sons, Ltd, pp. 229–248, accessed November 18, 2022, from https://onlinelibrary.wiley.com/doi/abs/10.1002/9781118829059.wbihms410.

Brown, A.K. & Peers, L. 2003, *Museums and Source Communities: A Routledge Reader*, Routledge, London and New York.

Bruchac, M. 2018, *Savage Kin: Indigenous Informants and American Anthropologists*, University of Arizona Press, Tucson.

Dirks, N. 1993, 'Colonial Histories and Native Informants: Biography of an Archive', in C.A. Breckenridge & P. van der Veer (eds), *Orientalism and the Postcolonial Predicament: Perspectives on South Asia*, University of Pennsylvania Press, Philadelphia, pp. 279–313.

Fforde, C., McKeown, T. & Keeler, H. (eds). 2020, *The Routledge Companion to Indigenous Repatriation: Return, Reconcile, Renew*, Routledge, Abingdon, Oxon.

Gibson, J. 2020, *Ceremony Men: Making Ethnography and the Return of the Strehlow Collection*, State University of New York Press, Albany.

Gibson, J. 2021, 'Aboriginal Secret-Sacred Objects, Their Values and Future Prospects', in H. Morphy, R. McKenzie, & R. McKenzie (eds), *Museums, Societies and the Creation of Value*, Routledge, London, pp. 103–122.

Gibson, J. & Batty, P. 2014, 'Reconstructing the Spencer and Gillen Collection Online: Museums, Indigenous Perspectives and the Production of Cultural Knowledge in the Digital Age', in H. Meyer, C. Schmitt, A-C. Shering, & S. Janssen (eds), *Corpora ethnographica online Strategien der Digitalisierung kultureller Archive und ihrer Präsentation im Internet*, Waxman, Munster, pp. 29–48.

Gibson, J.M. 2019, '"Factotum and Friend": Anthropologists, Informants and Ethnographic Exchange in Central Australia', *History and Anthropology*, pp. 1–29.

Gibson, J.M., Angeles, S. & Liddle, J. 2019, 'Deciphering Arrernte Archives: The Intermingling of Textual and Living Knowledge', in L. Barwick, J.A. Green, & P. Vaarzon-Morel (eds), *Archival Returns: Central Australia and Beyond*, Language and Documentation & Conservation Special Publication, University of Hawai'i Press, Honolulu, pp. 29–45, accessed from http://hdl.handle.net/10125/24876.

Glass, A. 2006, 'From Cultural Salvage to Brokerage: The Mythologization of Mungo Martin and the Emergence of Northwest Coast Art', *Museum Anthropology*, vol. 29, no. 1, pp. 20–43.

Golding, V. & Modest, W. 2013, *Museums and Communities: Curators, Collections and Collaboration*, Bloomsbury, London.

Hamilton, S. 2017, 'Sacred Objects and Conservation: The Changing Impact of Sacred Objects on Conservators', in G. Buggeln, C. Paine, & S.B. Plate (eds), *Religion in Museums: Global and Multidisciplinary Perspectives*, Bloomsbury Academic, London, pp. 135–146.

Hutchison, M. 2013, ' "Shared Authority" Collaboration, Curatorial Voice, and Exhibition Design in Canberra, Australia', in *Museum and Communities: Curators, Communities and Collaboration*, Bloomsbury Academic, London, pp. 143–162.

Jackson, M. 2013, *Lifeworlds Essays in Existential Anthropology*, The University of Chicago Press, Chicago.

Kakaliouras, A.M. 2012, 'An Anthropology of Repatriation: Contemporary Physical Anthropological and Native American Ontologies of Practice', *Current Anthropology*, vol. 53, no. S5, pp. S210–S221.

Keenan, S. 2017, 'The Gweagal Shield', *Northern Ireland Legal Quarterly*, vol. 68, no. 3, pp. 283–290.

Kirshenblatt-Gimblett, B. 1998, *Destination Culture: Tourism, Museums, and Heritage*, University of California Press, Berkeley.

Konishi, S., Nugent, M. & Shellam, T. (eds) 2015, *Indigenous Intermediaries: New Perspectives on Exporation Archives*, ANU Press and Aboriginal History Inc., Canberra.

Kreps, C. 2009, 'Indigenous Curation, Museums, and Intangible Cultural Heritage', in L. Smith & N. Akagawa (eds), *Intangible Heritage*, Routledge, London, pp. 193–209.

Krmpotich, C. & Peers, L. 2013, *This Is Our Life: Haida Material Heritage and Changing Museum Practice*, University of British Columbia Press, Vancouver.

Morphy, H. 1992, *Ancestral Connections: Art and an Aboriginal System of Knowledge*, University of Chicago Press, Chicago.

Morphy, H. 2020, *Museums, Infinity and the Culture of Protocols: Ethnographic Collections and Source Communities*, Routledge, London.

Myers, F. 2002, *Painting Culture: The Making of an Aboriginal High Art*, Duke University Press, Durham.

Nash, S.E. & Colwell-Chanthaphonh, C. 2010, 'Nagpra After Two Decades', *Museum Anthropology*, vol. 33, no. 2, pp. 99–104.

Nugent, M. & Sculthorpe, G. 2018, 'A Shield Loaded with History: Encounters, Objects and Exhibitions', *Australian Historical Studies*, vol. 49, pp. 28–43.

Onciul, B. 2015, *Museums, Heritage and Indigenous Voice: Decolonizing Engagement*, Routledge, New York.

Peers, L., Reinius, L.G. & Shannon, J. 2017, 'Introduction: Repatriation and Ritual, Repatriation as Ritual', *Museum Worlds*, vol. 5, no. 1, pp. 1–8.

Phillips, R.B. 2005, 'Re-Placing Objects: Historical Practices for the Second Museum Age', *The Canadian Historical Review*, vol. 86, no. 1, pp. 83–110.

Pickering, M. 2010, 'Despatches from the Front Line? Museum Experiences in Applied Repatriation', in P. Turnbull & M. Pickering (eds), *The Long Way Home: The Meaning and Values of Repatriation*, Berghahn Books, New York, pp. 163–174.

Russell, L. 2001, *Savage Imaginings: Historical and Contemporary Constructions of Australian Aboriginalities*, Australian Scholarly Publishing, Melbourne.

Silverman, R. (ed). 2015, *Museum as Process: Translating Local and Global Knowledges*, Routledge, London.

Smith, L.T. 1999, *Decolonizing Methodologies: Research and Indigenous Peoples*, Zed Books, Otago.

Thomas, N. 2018, 'A Case of Identity: The Artefacts of the 1770 Kamay (Botany Bay) Encounter', *Australian Historical Studies*, vol. 49, no. 1, pp. 4–27.

Thomas, N. 2019, 'What Are Museums Really for?' *Apollo*, accessed from www.apollo-magazine.com/defining-museums-in-the-21st-century/.

Timbery, B. 2020, 'Aboriginal History Told by Aboriginal People', accessed from www.gujaga.org.au/stories/aboriginal-history-told-by-aboriginal-people.

Tuck, E. & Yang, K.W. 2012, 'Decolonization Is Not a Metaphor', *Decolonization: Indigeneity, Education & Society*, vol. 1, no. 1, pp. 1–40.

Turnbull, P. & Pickering, M. (eds). 2010, *The Long Way Home: The Meaning and Values of Repatriation*, Berghahn Books, New York.

Turner, H. 2015, 'Decolonizing Ethnographic Documentation: A Critical History of the Early Museum Catalogs at the Smithsonian's National Museum of Natural History', *Cataloging & Classification Quarterly*, vol. 53, no. 5–6, pp. 658–676.

Tythacott, L. & Arvanitis, K. 2014, *Museums and Restitution: New Practices, New Approaches*, Ashgate, Farnham.

Wergin, C. 2021, 'Healing through Heritage? The Repatriation of Human Remains from European Collections as Potential Sites of Reconciliation', *Anthropological Journal of European Cultures*, vol. 30, no. 1, pp. 123–133.

# 2 Indigenous Appropriations of Anthropological Photography and Collections

'These *alyang* need a good song', Duncan Peltharre Lynch remarked as he held two boomerangs that had been collected by anthropologist Francis James Gillen in the 1890s. Flanked by three other Arrernte elders who had travelled to the Melbourne Museum to launch a website that hosted the collections Gillen and his anthropological collaborator Walter Baldwin Spencer, Lynch began to gently tap the objects together in time with the tune that he was quietly humming. Unsure whether the museum would permit the playing of these century-old objects, he looked gingerly across the room. His hesitation was, however, quickly allayed when the collection manager sensitively commented that, 'if these objects can't be used on occasions like this, then why have them at all?'

Once central to the endeavours of salvage anthropology, the collections of anthropologists – including objects such as these Arrernte boomerangs – have shifted in value and appreciation over the course of the twentieth century. Originally sought out as data to support the dominant evolutionary paradigm and notions of European superiority, the nature of these collections changed as the discipline of anthropology matured. By the end of the nineteenth century, anthropology had developed into a fieldwork-based discipline, favouring participant-observation and intensive fieldwork among living societies. Armchair theorising, evolutionism, and speculative histories were rejected as the data being gathered did not fit earlier evolutionary models. By the late twentieth century, the rise of postcolonial theory and increased Indigenous activism led to these collections being considered as either cultural appropriations or trophies of colonialism. The legacies and forms of value associated with these collections remain in flux.

Conserved and cared-for for over a century, many of the large and well-documented anthropological collections, such as those produced by Spencer and Gillen in Australia, but also Franz Boas in North America (Glass 2018; Glass, Berman & Hatoum 2017) and Alfred Cort Haddon in the Pacific (Herle & Philp 2020), have begun to take on new forms of value via novel engagements. In most cases, our understanding of these anthropological collections is being fundamentally reshaped by source-community interrogations

DOI: 10.4324/9781003158752-2

and fine-grained research into the histories of their production. In the final decades of the twentieth century, Indigenous peoples in many different settler-colonial settings came into museums with a series of ideas about the meaning of objects. Commenting on these experiences with Melanesians and Indigenous Australians, Lissant Bolton (2001) has noted that these engagements 'unsettled and irretrievably' altered the ways in which ethnographic collections could be imagined and understood. Increasingly valued as cultural heritage rather than anthropological data, these collections have come to be seen as reservoirs of social and cultural meaning for their source communities. Just as the Arrernte men at the Melbourne Museum were encouraged to hold objects and make music with them, Indigenous engagements with objects in most Australian museums are now celebrated and encouraged. Equally important to these changes, however, is the way that Indigenous people have come to appreciate these assemblages not simply as external, colonial vestiges, but as having an influence on the way they now perceive themselves. As anthropologist Fred Myers (2002, p. 12) has observed, these '*ur* representations' are now 'part of *their* world'. The materials amassed by various anthropologists, missionaries, collectors, and other documenters have had a lasting effect on the representation and reproduction of local cultures.

This chapter discusses the digital return and increased circulation of the collections of anthropologists Walter Baldwin Spencer and Francis Gillen, among Arrernte and Warumungu peoples in Central Australia. We begin with an analysis of how their extensive photographic collections have been appropriated to re-imagine public representations of local Aboriginal identity and discuss different creative responses. Greater access to this collection among both Arrernte and Warumungu communities has inspired artistic re-workings of anthropological photography, the re-centring of local Indigenous histories, and attempts to rethink anthropological collecting encounters through Indigenous cultural categories.

## Repurposing Anthropological Photography

In the history of Australian, indeed global, anthropology, the photographs of Spencer and Gillen have captured significant interest (Vium 2018; Kreinath 2012; Batty, Allen & Morton 2007; Banks 1998). The duo amassed an enormous collection of glass plate photographs via both their collaborative fieldwork and independently. Their most voluminous collections depicted elaborate Arrernte religious rituals, featuring complex ceremonial paraphernalia and dramatic performances. Though these photographs were made with the original intention of documenting primitive cultural life, I agree with Peterson that the complexity they conveyed instead worked to 'disrupt' simple evolutionary theories. The Arrernte were assumed to be humans in the 'chrysalis phase' of social evolution (Kuklick 2006); however, Spencer and Gillen's photographs presented contrary evidence of 'advanced sophisticates'

(Peterson 2006, p. 20). It is, therefore, hard to sustain the argument that the purpose of these photographs, which featured prominently in their publications and make up the bulk of their photographic collections, supported the Arrernte people's assumed place in an evolutionary hierarchy. The portraits they made of people, however, recorded different facial profiles and, along with Spencer's collection of hair samples and anthropometric measurements, were used to test theories of human evolution, development, and migration. Despite a far smaller component of their collection, these images reduced individual people to unnamed 'specimens' and were not intended as a way of remembering the personalities of the people they encountered, in the way that later anthropologists would do. They were ways of recording the variance between individuals in terms of personal appearance, different facial structures, and different types of frizzy, wavy, or straight hair, following a style of portraiture used by anthropologists of the late nineteenth and early twentieth centuries, whereby images of different side and front profiles would be made in an attempt to obtain examples of different 'racial types' (Lydon 2016a). Despite this framing, the descendants of those pictured have begun to find their own value in Spencer and Gillen's photographs.

The anthropological tomes of Walter Baldwin Spencer and Francis James Gillen (Spencer & Gillen 1899, 1904, 1927) and the distribution of their photographs and artefacts to colleagues and collecting institutions across the world had an enormous influence on how Aboriginal peoples were perceived globally. Within Central Australian Aboriginal communities too, copies of these photos were displayed by Gillen in public slide shows and kept by some individuals (Gillen 2001, pp. 91, 125, 157), and there was a general awareness of the contents of the publications among the community. In the 1930s, some of the men photographed discussed these images with anthropologist Olive Muriel Pink, and in 1929, Arrernte elder, Yerrampe, demonstrated his deep knowledge of the publications to the Hungarian Freudian anthropologist Géza Róheim (1974, p. 62). These books remained standard texts for newcomers to Central Australia, and reprints and facsimiles continue to be circulated.

It was only with the launch of the Spencer and Gillen website in 2013; however, the entirety of Spencer and Gillen's collections was made accessible online. Prior to this, small groups of Central Australian Aboriginal people would make the long and expensive journey to either the South Australian Museum or Melbourne Museums to see the bulk of Spencer and Gillen's collections. Kaytetye elder, Tommy Thompson, for example, showed me his carefully kept small collection of black and white photocopied photo prints, including several Spencer portraits of Kaytetye people made at Barrow Creek in 1901 (Figure 2.1), which he had acquired during a visit to the South Australian Museum many years before. Kept in a small shoe box, Thompson clearly cherished these items and had done a remarkable job of protecting them from the extreme desert environment and climate.

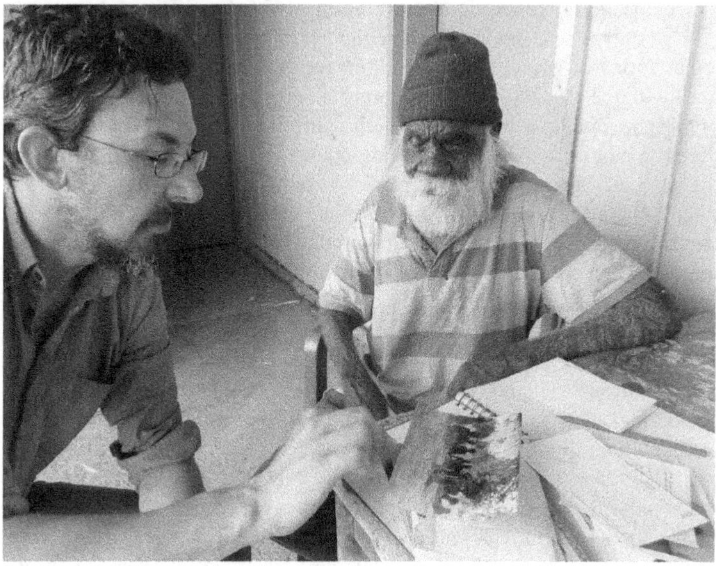

*Figure 2.1* Going over Tommy Thompson's photographic collection with him in 2017 (photo: M. Turpin).

For over a decade now, the Spencer and Gillen photographs, as well as their audio and film recordings, images, artefacts, and manuscripts, have been freely distributed in digital form to communities in an open-ended manner. Developed between 2009 and 2013, this digital reconstruction brings together objects collected by Spencer and Gillen, and distributed across 26 contributing institutions in Australia, the United States, and Europe. Users can search and browse material by institution, Indigenous language group, totem, place, and person; the site allows Aboriginal people and others to explore the history and contents of this distributed collection (Jones 2021, p. 33). The site has been accessed by over 68,000 users from Australia but also from the United States, France, Canada, and South America, but the most important users are Aboriginal people in Central Australia, who have readily taken to the site for their own purposes.

## Indigemoji and Spencer and Gillen

Increased discoverability and accessibility to these collections have led to important appropriations. As an example, in 2019, a series of Australian Indigenous 'picture characters' or pictograms, more commonly known as emojis, were produced for use on mobile phones by the Indigemoji project.

Developed in the township of Alice Springs with Arrernte people, the project's principal aim was to promote the Arrernte language, hand signs, and other forms of communication within the now ubiquitous mobile phone technology. Some of these emojis were based on Spencer and Gillen's portrait photographs. For the Indigemoji team, it was important to have features on mobile applications that raised awareness about people's ancestral links to the land and totemic species but also other aspects of everyday life, culture, and language.[1] This sentiment was echoed by a similar project developed from within the Haida communities of Canada around the same time, who made comparable emojis based on their own weaving and carving designs, ancestral stories, and language (Edenshaw 2020). As part of a now well-established tradition of Indigenous responses to a global infosphere (Ginsburg 1991; Dyson, Grant & Hendriks 2015), both the Haida Emoji Sticker App and the Indigemoji project sought to counteract global technological and cultural changes through the promotion of their own local cultures.

What made the Indigemoji project different from the Haidi project was its conscious engagement with colonial after-effects. Among images used in the application to represent contemporary Arrernte cultures, such as hand signs and facial expressions, Indigemoji also foregrounded a colonial history. This was done, first, via the inclusion of emojis that depicted locally significant totemic plant and animal species that have either become endangered or extinct due to environmental damage and the introduction of feral species. As developers of the application explained,

> a simple emoji of a bilby or a bandicoot promotes their memory, their name, their places in the landscape where they sprang into existence in the *Altyerre* [Dreaming], and where they moved about on their epic journeys. This way they remain in our landscape.[2]

The history of colonial encounters, however, was further evoked via the deliberate incorporation of the early colonial gaze via the appropriation of Spencer and Gillen's anthropological portraits. The two illustrated emojis for 'man' and 'woman' were drawn from two examples from Spencer and Gillen's portraits of Arrernte people as 'types'. Both photographs were chosen from the Spencer and Gillen corpus as it was felt that they best represented classical images of the Arrernte male and female genders.[3]

1 Indigemoji, www.indigemoji.com.au/ayeye-akerte-about.

2 Indigemoji, www.indigemoji.com.au/ayeye-akerte-about.

3 The male emoji is based on object XP14271. The original glass plate sleeve handwritten annotation states: 'Arunta (full)'. The original print caption: 'Arunta man. (Full). (See 1443). Alice Springs. 1896.'

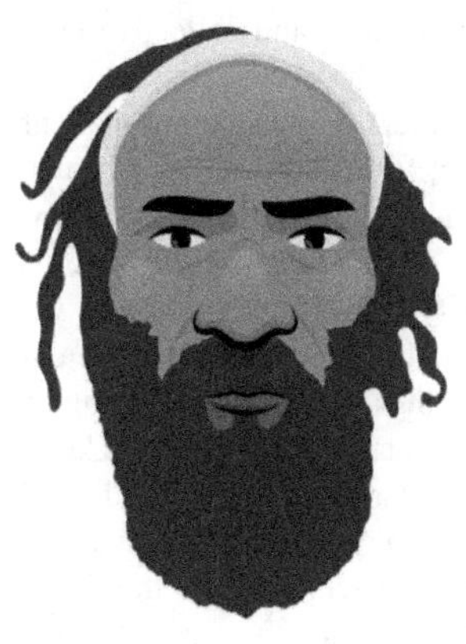
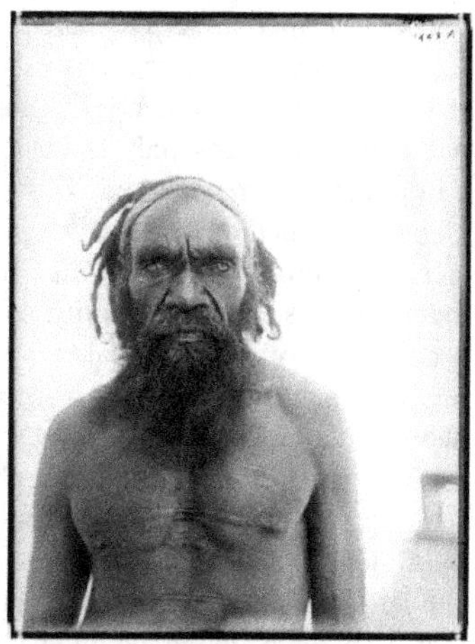

*Figure 2.2* The male Arrernte emoji and Spencer's photograph of an unnamed Arrernte man c.1896 (Melbourne Museum, Spencer Collection XP14271).

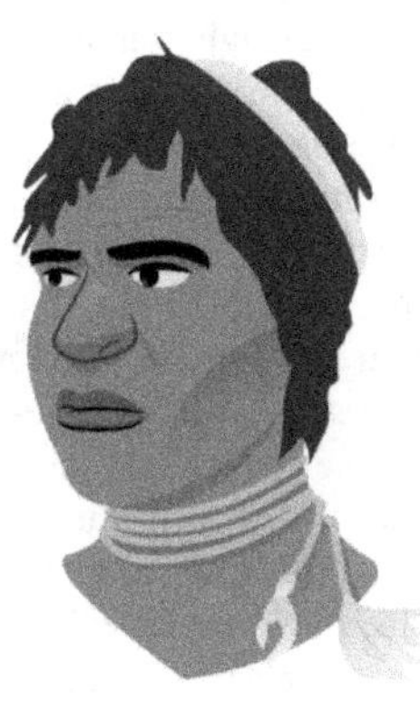
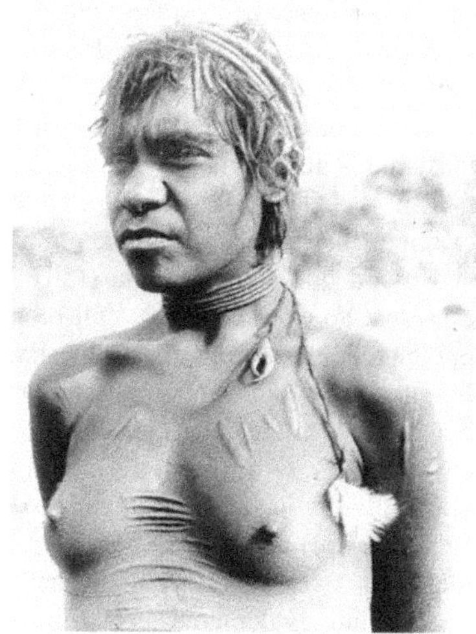

*Figure 2.3* The female Arrernte emoji and Gillen's photograph of an unnamed Arrernte woman c.1895 (South Australian Museum Collection).

Looking at these images today (Figures 2.2 and 2.3), we can see both the man and woman photographed adopt confident postures. Standing upright and seemingly self-assured, these individuals appear relaxed in front of

Spencer's camera. As such, there is little wonder that these images were chosen by the Indigemoji team as expressions of personal and collective pride among Central Australian Aboriginal people. The anthropological gaze of the photographs also ensured that characteristic markers of local Aboriginal cultural practice were captured. The Arrernte man, for example, is shown with a distinctive ochred hair-string headband, dread-locked hair, and decorative cicatrices across his chest, which all continue to be recognised as external indicators of seniority, authority, and masculinity. This same photograph was used in promotional materials for a large public celebration of Arrernte culture held at the *Mbantua Festival* in Alice Springs in 2013. In the original photograph, however, we see that Spencer has erected a white cloth backdrop to focus attention on the figure's physical characteristics, thus excluding all social, historical, and cultural contexts. The photograph of the woman, taken by Gillen, although including the environmental backdrop into the frame, similarly documents her traditional neck and hair adornments made of hair string, an eagle's talon, and a characteristic *alpeyt* (bilby tail tip) trimming. She stares away from the camera seemingly poised and resolute.

Having selected these anthropological portraits as ideal representations of Arrernte men and women, it was left to Aboriginal artist Graham Wilfred Jnr to adapt them into digital illustrations. These illustrations have since been described by the project as one small way of decolonising the Internet and have been shared across multiple global messaging applications (Sulikowski 2019). Their origin in early anthropological collecting, however, remains largely unknown to most users. The identities of these individuals also remain a mystery as neither Spencer nor Gillen recorded their names. The sleeve containing the original glass plate of the man, for example, features a sole annotation commenting on his tribal affiliation and blood quantum, 'Arunta (full)'. A reminder that this person was to represent an exemplar of a 'full-blood' Aboriginal person, meaning without mixed, non-Indigenous ancestry. The photo of the Arrernte woman is without any additional annotation, suggesting that the racial status of both was presumed to have long-term 'scientific' value. Contemporary engagements with Spencer and Gillen's photographs, however, reveal far more interest in the biographies and identities of these people (Bradley, Adgemis & Haralampou 2014), as well as their representational power as idealised Arrernte, rather than their 'racial purity'. Though the names of the individuals depicted were originally considered of little consequence to the anthropological project being undertaken, digital reproductions of their likeness now elicit feelings of distinctiveness and cultural pride. The way that Arrernte people now use these photographs is far removed from outmoded theoretical concerns. Networked digital technologies, the proliferation of digitised, online books, and increasing online access to museum collections have enabled a new Arrernte reconnection with these images that would have been unimaginable to the collectors.

## The Stuart Statue, Spencer, Gillen, and Irrapmwe

Access to these photographs has also come to play a part in debates regarding the colonial history and monuments. In 2015, the Alice Springs Town Council erected a 4-metre-high statue of the first colonial explorer to reach the centre of Australia, John McDouall Stuart. The statue depicts Stuart holding a rifle and was erected in one of the town's popular parks where Aboriginal people (Arrernte and visitors from elsewhere) commonly congregate to socialise. Stuart's role was immortalised in the naming of the highway that crosses the Australian continent from north to south (roughly the trajectory taken by the Spencer and Gillen expedition in 1901), as well as a monument erected in his honour in 1939 and the official naming of this park as Stuart Park. However, many in the community were opposed to yet another celebration of this figure of colonial history, particularly one brandishing a rifle, given the history of punitive expeditions and shootings. Opposition to the statue increased following the global Black Lives Matter protests of 2020, which included the defacement or damage of statues representative of colonialism.

Amid these growing global debates about the removal of monuments to colonial power and processes of 'truth-telling', Indigenous historian Pat Ansell Dodds called for the installation of a counter-statute to honour the Arrernte people. By 2022, the Lhere Artepe Aboriginal Corporation, the representative body of the Arrernte traditional owner groups of Alice Springs, began lobbying for the creation of a statue representing the Arrernte ancestor, Irrapmwe Peltharre (c.1820–1905). Featuring prominently in the publications, photographs, and archival collections of Spencer and Gillen, Irrapmwe's memory, however, is tightly bound to the colonial legacies of anthropology.

Irrapmwe, who was also known as King Charley or by his totemic name Ntyarlke, was a key informant to Spencer and Gillen at the end of the nineteenth century and provided enormous detail on Arrernte cultural practices, religion, and language. He first worked with Francis Gillen who had taken up the position of Alice Springs Telegraph Station Master in 1892 and later met Spencer during his visit to the region in 1894 and 1896, and again in 1901. Through Gillen, information and artefacts provided by Irrapmwe were sent to Spencer in Melbourne. Irrapmwe was also known as a good friend to the white settlers who invaded his country, welcoming them, guiding them to water sources, and generally working in concert with them. Yet, Irrapmwe's relationship with the settlers was not always cordial. Sometimes, like when Gillen sent Irrapmwe's sons to jail in South Australia, he protested bitterly against the unfair treatment and withdrew from Gillen (meaning that Gillen lost a key informant for his anthropology work), travelled away from the township, and cut off his hair and beard in mourning for his sons.

Present-day knowledge of Irrapmwe has much to do with his close associations with Gillen. Gillen's forays into anthropology were greatly aided by the generosity of Irrapmwe; although the two men had their disagreements,

Irrapmwe was willing to accept him as a younger brother (Gibson 2013). Gillen and Spencer had recognised Irrapmwe as the prominent leader of 'the Alice Springs group' at that time, and two photographs of him – a side on view and frontal view, as in the mode of 'racial types' – were featured in Figures 7 and 8 in their *Native Tribes of Central Australia* (Spencer & Gillen 1899, pp. 29, 31). While the Arrernte community remembers Irrapmwe through these records, his interactions with Spencer and Gillen were further memorialised through an important museum exhibit in the early 2000s. For a long time, the Melbourne Museum exhibited a dramatised film dialogue between Spencer and Irrapmwe in which Irrapmwe was depicted by an actor chastising Spencer for not appreciating his status as a 'professor' in his own culture. The actor playing Irrapmwe speaks in English, not his first language (Arrernte), and adopts a modern, postcolonial critique by making complaints about Spencer's adoption of racist tropes and displaying sacred religious objects in the museum. The dialogue script was later explained by its principal author, anthropologist John Morton, as:

> a central vehicle for making explicit the desire of Indigenous peoples to represent themselves, particularly in museums; the importance of the repatriation of cultural materials, with repatriation understood in its widest sense to include all forms of Indigenous control of, and access to, 'cultural property'; the representation and development of Aboriginality through complex appropriations of the key concept of 'The Dreamtime'; and the roles played by academic experts and Indigenous spokespeople in making policy in Indigenous affairs. These five matters are all addressed in the film, woven into a single narrative line.
>
> (Morton 2004, p. 56)

This landmark postcolonial pedagogical tool left its mark on museology in Australia, and the relationship between Spencer and Gillen's collecting and Arrernte identity continues to be enmeshed (Hendry 2005, pp. 26–55; Kowal 2019). The Arrernte community appreciated the re-centring of one of their elders as a 'professor' of equal measure to Spencer, and the exhibit has helped raise the profile of Irrapmwe as an important historical figure. Watching this film with Arrernte/Anmatyerr elder Malcolm Pengart in 2009, he commented that 'it was good that they made these two men level'. Arrernte researcher Joel Liddle Perrurle has taken a similar approach to the debates over the Stuart statue in Alice Springs. For him, a statue could be produced of Irrapmwe 'in dialogue with Spencer or Gillen' as a way of marking 'the sharing of spaces and the achievements of Aboriginal people in shared histories', rather than the celebration of the one-sided 'triumphs' of colonial exploration and annexation.

Exploring these ideas further, Liddle also produced an artwork based on a Spencer and Gillen photograph of Irrapmwe for the *Monumental in a small-town way*, a group art exhibition in 2019 (Figure 2.4). Curated by arts facilitator

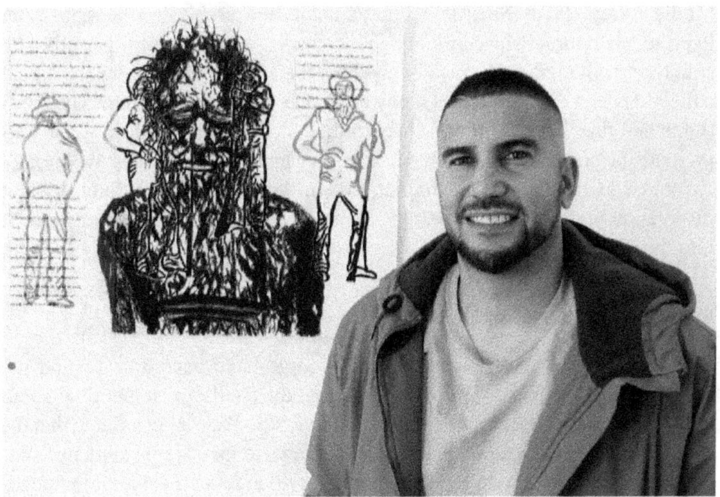

*Figure 2.4* Joel Liddle with his artwork depicting Arrernte elder Irrapmwe Peltharre overlaying sketch drawing of the colonial explorer John McDouall Stuart.

Judy Lovell and Arrernte elder Kathleen Wallace, the show promoted Indigenous and non-Indigenous collaborations as a way of responding to the Stuart monument, which they described as honouring 'the imperial achievements' of a Scottish explorer. Liddle's work is a tracing and charcoal redrawing of Spencer's image of Irrapmwe, who features prominently in the foreground, overshadowing four smaller hand-drawn outlines of the Stuart statue. A series of text panels are presented on either side of Irrapmwe detailing biographical and cultural information taken from anthropological archives and publications.

> The calligraphy writing in the background was taken from the biography of Irrapmwe on the Spencer and Gillen website. I made this artwork because I knew Irrapmwe had been lost in the mix a bit and people in our community didn't talk much about him. But Spencer and Gillen and other researchers recorded Irrapmwe Peltharre in their notes and collections as being the caterpillar boss of the areas we know as Mparntwe, Tyuretye, Anthwerrke etc. They show that he was the boss of the Alice Springs area, so I was paying a bit of reverence to his memory. I wanted to remind people that this was (and still is) caterpillar country. There was another boss – not John McDouall Stuart – around Alice Springs at the time Stuart came through in the 1860s. I also read that one of my own ancestors, a man named Urterre-arenye, remembered seeing Stuart crossing the Burt plain, when he was a young man.

Liddle's work takes Spencer's photographic and archival collections and, like the Melbourne Museum dialogue, creates a new historical narrative by countering colonial tropes head-on. This rebalancing, using anthropological collections and data, produces a powerful statement on the Arrernte people's rights and their deep ancestral links to the Alice Springs township that well pre-date the arrival of Stuart. In appropriating an image once used to objectify Arrernte identity, Liddle has found pride in these photographs, and through his interventions in research and art, he has been able to bring humanity back into the frame.

## Warumungu Responses

The relative ease with which Arrernte people have been able to find the humanity in Spencer and Gillen's photographs tells us something about the social relations that influenced their production. We cannot assume that the anthropologists coerced their subjects. There is, in fact, ample evidence suggesting otherwise. In one letter to Spencer, Gillen reveals some of the negotiations that took place when a group of men 'allowed him to photograph a Corroboree . . . in return for a blow out of flour, tea, and sugar'. Gillen 'accepted their terms, generously adding sundry half sticks of tobacco if their get up be satisfactory' (Gillen 2001, p. 97). These consultations are amply documented in Gillen's interactions with the Arrernte people over two decades, and a similar method was used during the duo's expedition across the continent in 1901, which exposed them to new Aboriginal people and communities unfamiliar with their interests and intentions. The photographs taken during this expedition, particularly those made of Kaytetye and Warumungu people, are suggestive of a similarly compassionate approach. Using the innovative Goertz-Anschutz camera with an extremely fast shutter speed (one-thousandth of a second), they were able to capture portraits quickly (Batty 2018, p. 50) that conveyed relaxed moments of interaction.

Warumungu artist Joseph 'Yugi' Jungarayi Williams is another Aboriginal person with a deep interest in this visual material. Williams grew up with knowledge of Spencer and Gillen's publications and specifically their *Northern Tribes of Central Australia* (1904), which included evidence that supported the Warumungu peoples' successful land claims around the Tennant Creek township in the 1980s. Unlike their Arrernte collecting, which was carried out sporadically over numerous fieldwork events (between 1894 and 1926), Spencer and Gillen spent only two months among the Warumungu at the Tennant Creek Telegraph Station. The extensive collection of boomerangs, coolamons, shields, axes, knives, and more magical and sacred items came together during an intensive period of trade and barter. It remains the largest of its kind for the Warumungu people and is a testament to their profuse and fervent material production.

Spencer's collecting photography during this time is now regarded as a transformative episode in the history of anthropology giving rise to a 'new form of ethnographic authority based on eyewitness testimony' (Bennett et al. 2017, p. 34). The published photos of Warumungu people, like those made of the Arrernte earlier, tended to obscure references to interactions with settler culture although there was now a greater inclusion of people wearing European clothes. Portraits of men who encountered and confronted explorers, and photographs of the Barrow Creek Telegraph Station, which was attacked in 1874, begin to narrate colonial conflict and imply domination over the local populace. Povinelli has written incisively about these fieldwork interactions, noting that 'one aspect of colonial power was being bracketed by another equal and opposing colonial force; that Spencer and Gillen were holding police, settlers, and starvation at bay' (2002, p. 94). Using their interactions with the anthropologists to their best advantage, Warumungu men and women present themselves before the cameras as a means of 'building a dialogic platform' (Bennett et al. 2017, p. 35) with the conquering Europeans.

This dialogic platform now has considerable resonance with the Warumungu people. As an artist of both Warumungu and Croatian ancestry, Williams has actively incorporated these photographs into his practice producing drawings of the Warumungu portraits (Figure 2.5). I first became aware of William's work when I read an article on his drawing practice as part of the Tennant Creek Brio (Finnane 2020). Drawing upon imagery associated with pre-colonial traditions of the Warumungu, everyday life in Tennant Creek, and historical and anthropological collections, Brio's objective is to produce works that thrive alongside 'Captain Cook culture', meaning the dominant Euro-Australian culture. 'We collect objects and materials that come from two different worlds . . . these materials tell stories about two different worlds crossing over'.[4] In William's case, he uses museum collections, schematic drawings of mining operations on Warumungu land, and intensive re-illustrations of Spencer's Warumungu photography to reveal something of the past overlaid in the present.

Williams became aware of the online collections of Spencer and Gillen in 2020 after being alerted to the site by non-Indigenous artist/documentary-painter Bevil Staley. Despite being already familiar with the small number of images published in *Northern Tribes of Central Australia* (1904), he would spend hours cross-examining the large online archives from his home in

4 ABC Arts Australia, Tennant Creek Brio at the Biennale of Sydney, *YouTube*, www.youtube.com/watch?v=Wehhsb5Raak.

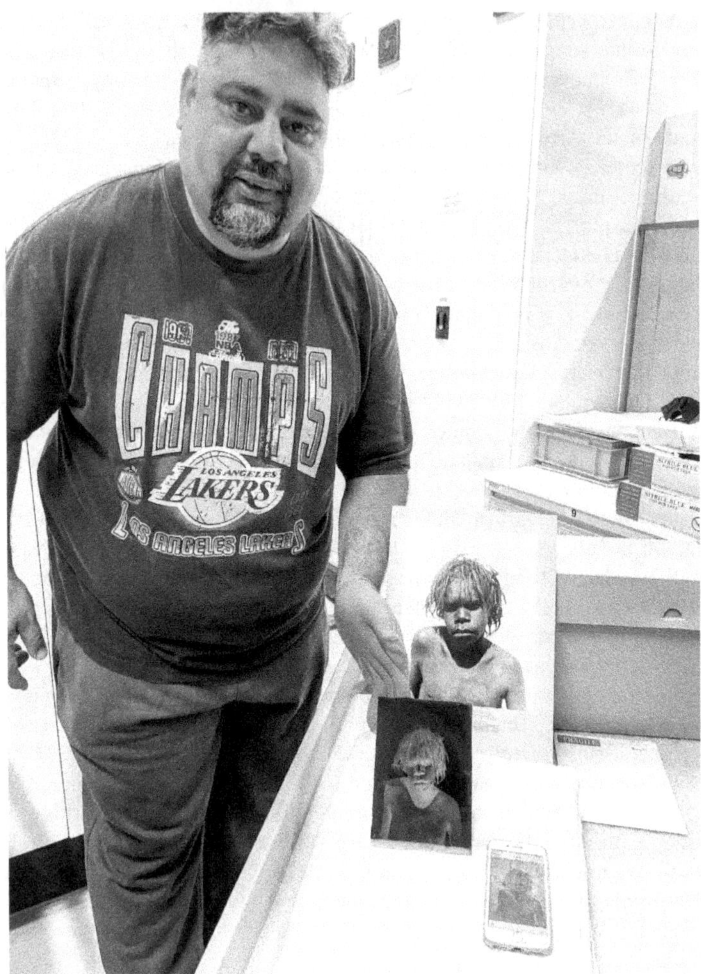


*Figure 2.5* Joseph Yugi Williams at the Melbourne Museum in 2022. He is holding an original Spencer glass plate of a Warumungu boy, a print of the same image, and a digital photograph of Williams' painting of this same image captured on his mobile phone.

Tennant Creek, over 2,000 km away from the Melbourne museums where the original glass plates are kept.

> I used that website all the time. Sometimes up to five times a day! But I was looking at those old photos before the website was even made. Me

> and a few other family members used to look at the original Spencer and Gillen books, they were really old and fragile. I used to work at the Central Land Council office in Tennant Creek and they had those books there. We used to photocopy those pictures and share them with family. That was before the website came along.[5]

Feeling 'very proud' to be able to 'look into the eyes of my ancestors', Williams considers the hundreds of photographs taken by the anthropologists as personally affecting. One photo, for example, portrays a man thought to be his mother's grandfather. Another depicts a woman who he says looks remarkably like his own mother. Celebrating the improved access to this visual material over time, Williams cherishes the opportunity to see each image within the context of the larger Spencer and Gillen corpus, and recognises their value to present generations. 'We all feel proud that these two white men came here and took photos of our people because we can now see that, and see that forever' (in Jonscher 2021). The digital recirculation of good-quality digital reproductions of these images has also greatly informed his own contemporary art practice, including the production of large-scale replica portraits:

> When I started doing my paintings, when I started painting the 'Old People', I used the website. I just googled 'Spencer and Gillen' and all our Old People came up then. Some of these men are grand old chaps. I save the images to my desktop and then print them out. The images are really good quality, which helps because I blow them up big on a projector and then trace them to get the right shape and proportions. I also put the smaller print outs next to me as I am painting.[6]

By taking these photographic objects and transforming them into celebrations of the Old People, William's work is part of a growing movement in Aboriginal Australia to de-associate these objects from their origins in racialised theory. Queensland Indigenous artist Vernon Ah Kee undertook a similar transformation of the photographic portraits taken by anthropologist Norman Tindale in the 1930s as part of his 2012 exhibition *Transforming Tindale* (see Lydon 2016b). Co-curated with Aboriginal scholar Michael Aird, the exhibition featured Ah Kee's response to photographs taken of Aboriginal people during Tindale's Queensland expeditions. Much like Williams and Liddle, Ah Kee produced his own large-scale illustrations of his relatives based on Tindale's photographs to remind audiences of their unique personalities and life histories. As a result, Ah Kee was able to de-centre the anthropological endeavour and maximise Indigenous individuality and experience.

5 Personal Communication with Joseph Williams 23/06/2021.

6 Personal Communication with Joseph Williams 23/06/2021.

The journey of discovering the Tindale collection and sharing with his family the extensive documentation associated with them, including his detailed genealogical records, became central to his and his community's re-engagement with the material. Ah Kee and his relations were also able to build an important collaboration with the South Australian Museum (which holds the Tindale archive) and the State Library of Queensland (which initially provided access to photocopies of the archive).

In a similar way, Joseph Williams is most drawn to objects with a connection to his relatives and interrogates collections to reconstruct local histories. This is not done in isolation. The oral memories of the Warumungu people underpin his engagements and are then used to augment the archival record. Any photographs or information pertaining to two men 'Zulu' and 'Cockney' are, for example, of particular interest because of the role they played in navigating relations along the colonial frontier. As their traditional country was chosen by authorities as a suitable site for a Telegraph Station in the late 1800s, these men had to contend with governmental reach but also acknowledge that their lands had become a significant nodal point of interaction between remote Aboriginal populations and settlers. Though Spencer or Gillen never named these men in their publications, they did mention them by name in their diaries and correspondence and on the reverse of a small number of photographic prints.[7] The archival record left by the anthropologists, for example, describes Zulu as 'a very intelligent Warramunga interpreter', and both Zulu and Cockney are noted by Gillen as expert informants.

Proud of these old men and the intermediary labour that they performed on behalf of their community, Williams uses the Spencer collection as a resource to be mined for details on these interactions. The story of Cockney, Williams' great grandfather on his mother's side, is of particular interest.

> Those two men, Zulu and Cockney, were the main informants to Spencer and Gillen and the two senior men for the Tennant Creek area. A lot of people in our community know about those two men. Cockney Jakkamarra was *jalajirppa* (white cockatoo) dreaming. He was my great grandfather, my mother's father's father.[8]

## Collecting and Mutual Obligations

Williams' interest in this collection has now evolved into a personal exploration of engagements with collectors and collecting spanning three generations. Not only is Williams the great grandson of an important informant

7 See item XP14282, Melbourne Museum. Also, Spencer's 1901 Personal Journal, 25 July, Camp 39, Tennants Creek.

8 Personal Communication with Joseph Williams 23/06/2021.

to Spencer and Gillen, but his grandfather (Cockney's son), 'Tracker' Nat Williams, was also a prolific maker of artefacts that were regularly gifted as a 'way of extending his authority into white society' (Jorgensen & Williams 2022). Known variously as 'Tracker Nat', Warano, or Nat Williams Juppurla, William's grandfather was a skilled maker of coolamons, spearthrowers, shields, and water carriers, often painting them with men dancing in ceremonial dress or hunting with boomerangs and spears. Tracker Nat openly traded in these products to garner attention and influence among white power brokers – missionaries, teachers, and government officials – in the 1940s and 1950s.

Tracker Nat objects are now being rediscovered by Joseph Williams and others across numerous Australian museum collections. Investigating this history with fervour, Williams has visited numerous Australian museums, regularly searches online auction sites, and is networked with scholars and collectors who have developed in interest in Tracker Nat's distributed oeuvre. Tracker Nat objects and drawings have now been identified in the Berndt Museum of Anthropology, the Melbourne Museum, the Queensland University Anthropology Museum, and the South Australian Museum, as well as numerous private collections. While many of these objects have been catalogued without attribution to Tracker Nat, his style is unmistakable, and Williams is now working with museums and other collecting institutions to ensure proper acknowledgement. In October 2022, for example, I stumbled across an unattributed Tracker Nat shield at the University of Queensland Anthropology Museum (Figure 2.6), which has now been added to a growing catalogue of Tracker Nat productions.

Unearthing these histories of Cockney and Tracker Nat through collections access and research has enabled Joseph Williams to generate an important story of Warumungu's engagement and agency. As a third-generation Warumungu family member to make artefacts and art to engage with wider society, Joseph Williams understands these exchanges as deeply rooted in the

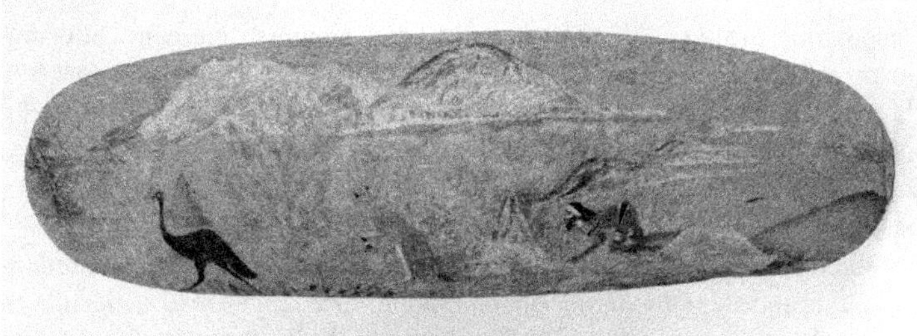

*Figure 2.6* Painted shield attributed to Tracker Nat Williams depicting Warumungu hunter approaching a red kangaroo and an emu (University of Queensland Anthropology Museum, Acc. 2040. Photo: Carl Warner).

distinctive Warumungu concept of *ngijinkirri*. Understood as a performance of the mutual obligation, *ngijinkirri* involves a process of giving and receiving objects and information to generate social bonds. William's position is that, while non-Indigenous collectors may not have recognised it, *ngijinkirri* or 'mutual gifting' was always central to these interactions from a Warumungu perspective. The intention is to implicate 'the giver and receiver into a relationship of obligation' (Williams, McLean & Jorgensen Forthcoming). Relationships like this have been observed elsewhere in Central Australia, where, in contrast to Western law with its strong protections for personal property, Aboriginal customary law tends towards 'mutual borrowing', a practice that intends to bring people together as 'closely cooperating kin' (Myers 1986, p. 111).

Seen through the lens of *ngijinkirri*, the history of collecting takes on new significance. When a recipient, be it an individual collector or a museum, receives an object, they open themselves up to continuing relationships and responsibilities. Williams suggests that categories such as *ngijinkirri* have been integral to Warumungu interactions with outsiders, challenging the framing of colonial encounters from solely Western historical or theoretical perspectives. His examinations of the Spencer and Gillen online collections, as well as his uncovering of Tracker Nat's objects and diplomacy, are critically shaped by Warumungu cultural concepts and interpretative frameworks. *Ngijinkirri* urges us to see collecting events as attempts to ameliorate power imbalances and endure in the face of hardship but also build connections between Warumungu people and outsiders over three generations. We might then ask how collectors, and by extension the museums that now possess these objects, might honour these relationships? Were these intentions misunderstood or ignored? What might be given in exchange for Warumungu collaboration? How might the call to be closely cooperating kin be answered?

## Conclusion

Responding to these questions in a way that honours divergent collection histories is now part of the difficult burden of museums everywhere. While the Arrernte men mentioned at the beginning of this chapter only briefly gave life to their ancestor's boomerangs at the Melbourne Museum, the photographs collected of Arrernte and Warumungu people have been disseminated and used by descendants in a myriad of ways. This does not mean, however, that the return of anthropological collections to source communities ought to rely upon digital dissemination. In 2022, a small collection of Warumungu objects collected by Spencer and the Tennant Creek telegraph operator, James Field (a cousin to Gillen by marriage), were repatriated following careful negotiations between the Australian Institute of Aboriginal and Torres Strait Islander Studies (AIATSIS) and the Tamaki Paenga Hira

Auckland War Memorial Museum in Aotearoa/New Zealand. A group of Warumungu people, including Joseph Williams, spent over a year consulting with the museum and concluded that, although the objects had been 'freely given by community members to visiting collectors', their return would foster fair relations between all parties.[9] The principal objective is *ngijinkirri*.

These Warumungu objects now join many others from the Spencer and Gillen collection that has been on permanent loan to the Nyinkka Nyunyu Art and Culture Centre in Tennant Creek from the Melbourne Museum since 2003. Described by the Warumungu community as *wurrmulalkki* (returned histories), these objects are proudly displayed at the cultural centre alongside Spencer and Gillen's black and white photographs and interpreted through the frame of long engagements with collectors, anthropologists, and collecting institutions (Nyinkka Nyunyu Art and Culture Centre 2003). As seen in the appropriation of Spencer and Gillen's photographs, objects borne from colonial observation, measurement, and extraction are still readily used in creative acts of defiance and pride. The dialogic aspects of anthropological collection-making are evident, if not always made explicit. Similarly, Spencer and Gillen's portrait photography, despite its original intention to inform racial anthropometric studies, evidently exudes affective qualities that affirm Arrernte and Warumungu reinterpretations. As Elizabeth Edwards has cogently argued, there 'is no linear trajectory' for these photos 'but a folding together of anthropology's own pasts and presents, for better or worse, with the pasts and presents of other people' (Edwards 2015, p. 248).

Reminiscent of how native scholars in North America are now 'salvaging the salvage anthropologists' (Warren & Barnes 2018), the recirculation and appropriation of Australian anthropological collections in recent years have aided the production of new forms of knowledge. The salvage anthropologists of the late nineteenth and twentieth centuries undoubtedly approached these communities during a time of vulnerability and loss, and they assumed a path of cultural decline, but the collections that they amassed are appreciated as important cultural and historical repositories. Peoples' appropriations of these assemblages have not produced a total break with colonialism but an 'ambiguous struggling through and with colonial pasts' to make 'different futures' (Brus & Zillinger 2021, p. 21). As their most avid excavators of these collections, Arrernte and Warumungu people treat these collections as shared intellectual spaces, as containing entangled histories of dominance and control but also as harbouring the seeds of collaboration, creativity, and curiosity.

9 Australian Institute of Aboriginal and Torres Strait Islander Studies, https://aiatsis.gov.au/whats-new/news/four-warumungu-objects-return.

## References

Banks, M. 1998, 'Visual Anthropology: Image, Object and Interpretation', in *Image-based Research*, Routledge, London.

Batty, P. 2018, 'Assembling the Ethnographic Field: The 1901–02 Expedition of Baldwin Spencer and Francis Gillen', in M. Thomas & A. Harris (eds), *Expeditionary Anthropology Teamwork, Travel and the 'Science of Man'*, Berghahn Books, New York, pp. 37–63.

Batty, P., Allen, L. & Morton, J.A. (eds). 2007, *The Photographs of Baldwin Spencer*, Miegunyah Press, Carlton, Victoria.

Bennett, T., Cameron, F., Dias, N., Dibley, B., Harrison, R., Jacknis, I. & McCarthy, C. 2017, *Collecting, Ordering, Governing: Anthropology, Museums, and Liberal Government*, Duke University Press, Durham.

Bolton, L. 2001, 'The Object in View: Aborigines, Melanesians, and Museums', in A. Rumsey & J. Weiner (eds), *Emplaced Myth, Space, Narrative, and Knowledge in Aboriginal Australia and Papua New Guinea*, University of Hawai'i Press, pp. 215–232, accessed June 1, 2021, from www.jstor.org/stable/j.ctvvn7zh.14.

Bradley, J., Adgemis, P. & Haralampou, L. 2014, ' "Why Can't They Put Their Names?": Colonial Photography, Repatriation and Social Memory', *History and Anthropology*, vol. 25, no. 1, pp. 47–71.

Brus, A. & Zillinger, M. 2021, 'Introduction: Transforming the Post/Colonial Museum', *Zeitschrift für Kulturwissenschaften*, vol. 15, no. 2, pp. 11–28.

Dyson, L.E., Grant, S. & Hendriks, M. 2015, *Indigenous People and Mobile Technologies*, Routledge, London.

Edenshaw, J. 2020, 'This Space Here', *BC Studies*, no. 205, pp. 7–10.

Edwards, E. 2015, 'Anthropology and Photography: A Long History of Knowledge and Affect', *Photographies*, vol. 8, no. 3, pp. 235–252.

Finnane, K. 2020, 'Desert Aboriginal Art Centres Adapt to the Pandemic', *Artlink*, vol. 40, no. 2, pp. 101–109.

Gibson, J. 2013, 'Addressing the Arrernte: FJ Gillen's 1896 Engwura Speech', *Australian Aboriginal Studies*, vol. 1, pp. 57–72.

Gillen, F.J. 2001, *'My Dear Spencer': The Letters of F.J. Gillen to Baldwin Spencer*, Hyland House Publishing Pty Limited, Flemington.

Ginsburg, F. 1991, 'Indigenous Media: Faustian Contract or Global Village?' *Cultural Anthropology*, vol. 6, no. 1, pp. 92–112.

Glass, A. 2018, 'Drawing on Museums: Early Visual Fieldnotes by Franz Boas and the Indigenous Recuperation of the Archive', *American Anthropologist*, vol. 120, no. 1, pp. 72–88.

Glass, A., Berman, J. & Hatoum, R. 2017, 'Reassembling The Social Organization: Collaboration and Digital Media in (Re)making Boas's 1897 Book', *Museum Worlds*, vol. 5, no. 1, pp. 108–132.

Hendry, J. 2005, *Reclaiming Culture: Indigenous People and Self-Representation*, Palgrave Macmillan, Basingstoke.

Herle, A. & Philp, J. (eds). 2020, *Recording Kastom: Alfred Haddon's Journals from the Torres Strait and New Guinea, 1888 and 1898*, Sydney University Press, Sydney.

Jones, M. 2021, *Artefacts, Archives, and Documentation in the Relational Museum*, Routledge, London.

Jonscher, S. 2021, 'Tennant Creek Artist Joseph Williams Learns New Techniques with Vivid Portraits of Ancestors', *ABC*, accessed from www.abc.net.au/news/2021-06-12/tennant-creek-artist-joseph-williams-indigenous/100205540?fbclid=IwAR3a16tOG3Lx2u4HdV12SEUba1rRkqTHDSEz4nsqRCEA83_zok-pWtMislo.

Jorgensen, D. & Williams, J. 2022, 'Rediscovering the Art of Tracker Nat: "The Namatjira of Carving"', *The Conversation*, accessed from https://theconversation.com/rediscovering-the-art-of-tracker-nat-the-namatjira-of-carving-184749?fbclid=IwAR3GzAqYqH7fAho5upKxduHc2lSs_YhJy3sNj2Cs90CRyhokNIonXaJWKcI.

Kowal, E. 2019, 'Spencer's Double: The Decolonial Afterlife of a Postcolonial Museum Prop', *BJHS Themes*, pp. 55–77.

Kreinath, J. 2012, 'Discursive Formation, Ethnographic Encounter, Photographic Evidence: The Centenary of Durkheim's Basic Forms of Religious Life and the Anthropological Study of Australian Aboriginal Religion in His Time', *Visual Anthropology*, vol. 25, no. 5, pp. 367–420.

Kuklick, H. 2006, '"Humanity in the Chrysalis Stage": Indigenous Australians in the Anthropological Imagination, 1899–1926', *British Journal for the History of Science*, vol. 39, no. 4, pp. 535–568.

Lydon, J. 2016a, 'Transmuting Australian Aboriginal Photographs', *World Art*, vol. 6, no. 1, pp. 45–60.

Lydon, J. 2016b, '"Real Photos": Transforming Tindale and the Postcolonial Archive', *Public History Review*, vol. 23, pp. 56–73.

Morton, J. 2004, '"Such a Man Would Find Few Races Hostile": History, Fiction and Anthropological Dialogue in the Melbourne Museum', *Arena Journal*, no. 22, pp. 53–71.

Myers, F.R. 1986, *Pintupi Country, Pintupi Self: Sentiment, Place and Politics Among Western Desert Aborigines*, University of California Press, Berkley.

Myers, F.R. 2002, *Painting Culture: The Making of an Aboriginal High Art*, Duke University Press, Durham.

Nyinkka Nyunyu Art and Culture Centre. 2003, *Wurrmulalkki: Returned Histories*, Nyinkka Nyunyu Art and Culture Centre, Tennant Creek.

Peterson, N. 2006, 'Visual Knowledge: Spencer and Gillens use of Photography in The Native tribes of Central Australia', *Australian Aboriginal Studies*, vol. 1, pp. 12–22.

Povinelli, E.A. 2002, *The Cunning of Recognition: Indigenous Alterities and the Making of Australian Multiculturalism*, Duke University Press, Durham.

Róheim, G. 1974, *Children of the Desert: The Western Tribes of Central Australia,* W. Muensterberger (ed), Basic Books, New York.

Spencer, S.B. & Gillen, F.J. 1899, *The Native Tribes of Central Australia*, Dover Publications, New York.

Spencer, S.B. & Gillen, F.J. 1904, *The Northern Tribes of Central Australia*, MacMillan and Co, London.

Spencer, S.B. & Gillen, F.J. 1927, *The Arunta: A Study of a Stone Age People*, Macmillan and Company, Limited, London.

Sulikowski, M. 2019, 'Giving Indigenous Australians a Visual Voice with Indigemoji', *Telstra Exchange*, accessed from https://exchange.telstra.com.au/giving-indigenous-australians-a-visual-voice-with-indigemoji/.

Vium, C. 2018, 'Temporal Dialogues: Collaborative Photographic Re-enactments as a Form of Cultural Critique', *Visual Anthropology*, vol. 31, no. 4–5, pp. 355–375.

Warren, S. & Barnes, B. 2018, 'Salvaging the Salvage Anthropologists: Erminie Wheeler-Voegelin, Carl Voegelin, and the Future of Ethnohistory', *Ethnohistory*, vol. 65, no. 2, pp. 189–214.

Williams, J., McLean, L. & Jorgensen, D. Forthcoming, 'Tracker Nat's Art of Ngijinkirri, the Tennant Creek Brio, Masonic Hand Signs and Warramungu History'.

# 3 Putting Objects Back in Place

Implied in the rhetoric of cultural repatriation is the notion that objects will return to their proper or rightful place. This is usually explained as sending objects 'home' or, in the parlance of Aboriginal Australia, seeing that they are 'back on country'. This relationship between place and object is critical to the process of cultural heritage repatriation. When museum and archival objects are removed from storeroom shelving, cabinets, and exhibition display cases, and re-engaged with by source communities, they are almost always made anew through processes of transfer and relocation. What is often left under-theorised, however, is the changing nature of 'home' and the different colonial inheritances that alter both the people and places where objects were originally collected from.

In this chapter, I re-examine this idea by assessing whether, in fact, objects can ever really return to a correct or unchanged position or place and how 'putting things in their place' – although a well-intentioned objective – can be less than straight forward proposition. Similarly, the idea that Indigenous communities or territories are invariable and stable locales also needs rethinking. The assumption of a smooth transition of cultural heritage back into place can be scrutinised by highlighting how objects and places, as well as the social and cultural contexts that make sense of them – including the mythological framework of the Dreaming and genealogical memory (see Sansom 2006) – are transformed over time. As this chapter demonstrates, the act of putting objects back into place can lead to wonderful and novel cultural responses and instigate new, productive relationships but, at the same time, raise new tensions. This is not surprising, given that, as phenomenologist Edward Casey has argued, human perception necessitates that we are 'never without emplaced experiences . . . not only in places but of them . . . and along with other entities on earth – are ineluctably place-bound' (1996, p. 19).

The centrality of place to Central Australian Aboriginal ontology was made apparent to me when I began returning digital copies of historical photographs to communities. Working for what was then known as the Northern Territory Library's *Indigenous Knowledge Centres* programme, I had negotiated access to suitable collections that could be digitised for return to the Anmatyerr

DOI: 10.4324/9781003158752-3

Library and Knowledge Centre in the community of Ti Tree in Central Australia. A small collection of photographs from the State Library of South Australia (SLSA) concerning the earliest missionary to live on Anmatyerr lands, Miss Annie Lock, was among the first to be returned. As soon as I began reviewing the black and white images with community members, there was an immediate call to re-visit the sites depicted.

The re-entry of these photographs into the community inspired a string of related activities centring on elders taking younger people to these sites to explain the history of the mission. Big Billy Woods Mpetyan, at that time, the senior traditional owner for the Ti Tree Well area (Nthwerey Pwerray), wanted the SLSA to know (and record in their catalogue) the Anmatyerr name for the place where the photographs were taken, Mer Ilpereny. Following Woods' lead, others began to move away from discussing the history of Annie Lock, who had only lived at the site for little over a year, and instead commented on the deeper ancestral connections that Anmatyerr families had to the place and the different *anengkerr* (Dreamings) that animated the landscape. To properly understand this, a visit to the site was organised. Other sites of local historical and cultural importance were pointed out, including various landforms created by ancestors, dwellings made by pastoralists in the mid-twentieth century, and, finally, the soakage (water source) where Lock had camped. In the sandy, dry riverbed at Mer Ilpereny, we examined the archival photos and discussed the importance of photographic repatriation as a source of 'memory'. The physical act of returning to the place, with photographic prints at-hand, surfaced a depth of local, cultural knowledge.

I later came to learn that this ushering of returned objects to their places of connection was a natural progression for people in Central Australia. Being in, being shown, and travelling to places in this part of Australia are central to 'the possibility of knowing', as other anthropologists have observed (Carty 2021, p. 2). The connections between places, people, animals, plants, stories, ancestors, and other non-human entities form the 'relational ontology' (Porr 2018) that underpins meaning-making within this sociocultural milieu. From this perspective, meaning is found within the *relationships* between entities in contrast to the so-called 'Western' knowledge, which deals with abstract, disembodied ideas, categorical distinctions, and often binary oppositions between things and persons, nature and culture, mind and body, and so on (Tilley 2004, p. 20). While the basic contention of a relational ontology is that the relations between entities are more fundamental than the entities themselves, in Australian Indigenous thinking, 'country' – meaning land, place, and home (see Sutton 1995) – does, however, take on a degree of prominence. Arrernte elder M. K. Turner (2010) has, for example, written that 'everything' emerges from 'Apmereyanhe', the 'Country Ground'. She suggests that knowledge can only ever be acquired through enmeshments grounded in place. When considering the return of cultural heritage, we need to examine how objects are positioned within this nexus of relationships, especially in relation to place. As will be illustrated later, making these connections is often the first step in seeing objects re-integrated.

## The Importance of Place

Across Aboriginal Australia, a person's relationship to the land is considered vital to conceptions of personal and cultural identity. As evidenced throughout the anthropological literature (Sutton 1995; Hercus, Hodges & Simpson 2002) and as expressed by Indigenous artists and authors (Turner 2010; Kean 2023), the interconnections between person, land, and myth are now well known. Critical to people's conception of place, however, is the presence of eternal ancestral beings in the land. During a process commonly known as Dreaming, ancestral beings created the world, left physical traces of their journeys, and brought forth the eternal essence of all things. Almost every feature of the landscape can, therefore, be explained as having been formed by these ancestral actions, and many place names will feature a reference to the movements, pursuits, and behaviours of the ancestors.

Research concerning the nature of these connections in different parts of Australia has been a feature of Australian anthropological discourse for decades (Peterson & Long 1986; Keen 1997; Harvey 2002). Place associations are also diverse across Australia. However, for the purposes of this chapter, it is sufficient to say that both specific sites and geographic regions evoke specific forms of meaning, obligation, and responsibility. In Central Australia, a person is said to be 'from' a particular place, meaning that they and their ancestors have resided in and spiritually emanated from specific locations, dating back many generations into the mythological eternal presence of the Dreaming. A person's spiritual Dreaming ancestor may, for example, be embodied in a certain feature of the landscape – say a tree, rock, a hill, or soakage. This fine-grained association links a person's identity in a rich and particular way. Individuals can also receive certain associations to 'country' through maternal or paternal inheritance. The activities of Dreaming ancestors who made the country are expressively recounted in song, dance, and storytelling repertoires or represented through objects or ceremonial designs. This knowledge is then shared across groups and along individual lines of kinship although specific meanings and associations may be highly valued and closely guarded as 'secret-sacred'.

Within museum catalogues, conceptions of place are far less refined. The typical rubric of 'provenance', which seeks to record the history of an object's ownership and movement over time, fails to capture this cultural complexity. Basic provenance research is still at a very preliminary stage for most Australian Aboriginal museum collections, many of which linger in stores under definitions of 'unprovenanced' or attributed to unworkable regional designations, such as 'southeastern Australia', 'Cape York', and the like. In North America too, Phillips (2005, p. 94) noted how community leaders remarked that, if museums cannot provide basic information about the attribution of objects in their collections, they have no right to continue as custodians. As critically important as ascertaining 'provenance' is in this form, Indigenous curator Gaye Sculthorpe argues it is 'only the beginning of a conversation' (2019, p. 277). Knowing that an object or a cache of objects was collected from a particular township is significant, but it may not tell us each item's cultural relationship to particular places, peoples, and stories, information that is too often absent from catalogues and (if available) found only within ancillary collection documentation. Bringing contemporary source community knowledge to bear on these ethnographic collections, alongside expertise in material culture and social and cultural anthropology, is, therefore, urgent to glean more detailed interconnections between place, people, and objects.

Despite important lessons being learned in recent decades, particularly as the eight major state museums in Australia have repatriated over 2,200 sacred objects since the mid-1980s (Pickering 2015; Anderson 1995; DoCA 2019, p. 2), collecting institutions, more generally, are only now at the cusp of grappling with Indigenous ways of understanding place. As John Carty from the South Australian Museum has stated, the prospect of 'country' is now 'the central museological challenge' emerging out of ongoing consultations with Indigenous groups in Australia (2019, p. 390). Carty uses consultations undertaken by the National Museum of Australia with the Gunditjmara people in south-west Victoria, which he was a part of, as an example. The museum's curators had taken booklets containing images and information about Gunditjmara material back to the community and wanted to discuss each object and its exhibition potential with the group. The community, on the other hand, politely leafed through the booklets before indicating that their priority was to take the curators into the country.

> The country itself, far more than any object in a museum or in a booklet, was the evidence that Gunditjmara presented for their culture and their identity . . . this was what people needed to see. In this context the objects that the museum was showing people seemed like pale abstractions, like somebody else's idea of culture.
>
> (Carty 2019, p. 391)

Country comes first and gives meaning to everything on it.

## Mapping Objects

In 2014, I was part of a repatriation project involving the Melbourne Museum and the Museum of Central Australia's Strehlow Research Centre (located in Alice Springs). The project had been co-designed by two Arrernte researchers, Mark Inkamala and Shaun Angeles, and sought to map over 300 objects collected by Mounted Constable Charles Ernest Cowle at the beginning of the twentieth century. The project had grown out of a meeting between curators from each of the nation's largest state museums and 20 Aboriginal cultural leaders from Central Australia. The objective of the meeting was to find ways of advancing the repatriation of Central Australian sacred objects, including many poorly provenanced items that required further investigation. At the conclusion of the meeting, a formal request was put to each of the state museums that their catalogue data be shared with the Strehlow Research Centre so that research could be pursued by Inkamala and Angeles at the local level.

With detailed collection data in the hands of the relevant Aboriginal researchers, it was hoped that they could develop an 'insiders' perspective on how each museum's collection of sacred objects had been catalogued and the links between them made. For example, the Melbourne Museum, the South Australian Museum, and the Strehlow Research Centre each held objects pertinent to notable Arrernte estates, as different generations of collectors had amassed objects from places close to Alice Springs and subsequently deposited them with different state institutions. The research objective was to try and reconstruct linkages between objects that had been separated through historical collecting processes. A key method to achieve this was to map object relationships to place.

The project began with sharing of data from the Melbourne Museum and a focus on the Ernest Cowle Collection. Cowle's collection includes 363 ethnographic objects, including over 100 sacred objects that had been sent to the director of the National Museum of Victoria, Professor Walter Baldwin Spencer, and donated to the museum between 1901 and 1903. Cowle had corresponded with Spencer for close to nine years and appreciated having his observations in natural science and ethnography taken seriously by the professor (see Mulvaney, Petch & Morphy 2000). As a colonial-era Mounted Police Officer, Cowle was prejudiced against Aboriginal people and routinely used whipping and other forms of violence on his Aboriginal prisoners although he did oppose murder unlike some of his predecessors (particularly constables Wilshire and Wirmbrandt). His correspondence with Spencer reveals a man with a genuine interest in Aboriginal cultural life, and the documentation that he produced for his ethnographic collection similarly exhibits a desire for detail and depth.

As we began to work through these previously unexamined notes, we came to realise that the details that he obtained from numerous informants could only have been gathered via prolonged cross-cultural dialogue. The information captured by Cowle, including careful summaries of object relationships to over 100 specific places and sacred sites, presented an opportunity to reconnect these significant objects with their present-day custodians. We began with an examination of the museum's electronic catalogue (known as Emu) to see how Cowle's commentary on Dreaming narratives and key cultural sites associated with each object had been made to fit the system. Most of the catalogue entries followed the usual practice of noting 'provenance', meaning where the objects had been assembled by the collector, in this case at the police outpost of Illamurta Springs. Each object's specific relationship to sites, which had been recorded by Cowle, had not been entered.

Understanding an object's individual place relationships would later become essential for determining who would need to be consulted regarding potential repatriation. In many cases, the documentation associated with ethnographic objects can be depressingly paltry; however, in Cowle's notes, we discovered extraordinary information that is now considered essential to producing meaning in a relational ontological context. His documentation not only included the names and personal totemic associations of the individuals who had sold items to him but also the Dreaming narratives related to each object, which often recounted the paths of ancestors as they moved between numerous named places. Knowing which ancestral narratives and places were linked to each object meant consultations could be had with present-day peoples associated with specific sites.

Cowle's notes had been used by museum registrars decades earlier to capture the kind of 'skeleton data' needed to accession each object. Common fields, such as 'Collector', 'Provenance', and 'Cultural Group' – meaning the associated Aboriginal language and cultural groups – had been ascribed, but Cowle's long narratives on an object's cultural significance had not always been added to the database's 'Primary' or 'Secondary Comments' fields. The challenge of capturing distinctive Indigenous knowledge categories in ways that make them useful within museum databases, and elevating them beyond the domain of a miscellaneous free text dump, is highlighted by Hannah Turner in her *Cataloguing Culture: Legacies of Colonialism in Museum Documentation* (2020). Cataloguers struggle to find ways of incorporating different perspectives into Museum database fields, which have their roots in earlier iterations of cataloguing and Western science. These electronic systems were not, for example, designed to account for Indigenous conceptions of place, whereby sites might reside within larger Countries (or estates) and be crisscrossed by ancestral stories with links to contemporary generations of people.

To Inkamala and Angeles, it was precisely this type of information that was essential to each object's classification, not an addendum to it, although several workarounds were trialled, such as attaching lengthy written narratives to each object or shoe-horning relational connections between pre-existing fields to mimic some of these cultural relationships. Despite these attempts, the relational ontologies of central Aboriginal Australians were poorly served by the database. Indigenous perspectives and knowledge had, of course, never been part of the elemental design of an Australian museum digital catalogue, and including this detail as part of a free-text narrative field, as Turner (2020, p. 191) argues, does little to change 'the nomenclature of objects' or help reframe objects 'in a meaningful way'. It was decided that geolocating each object's relationship to sites via digital mapping would be a useful way of visualising these vital relationships. Our team began plotting the known places recorded by Cowle using Google Earth. Locating and plotting European place names were relatively straightforward exercises; however, mapping Arrernte places, which have never been included in any authoritative register, was less straight forward. It required recruiting Arrernte cultural expertise across different regions and careful cross-referencing with the ethnographic literature.

Even where the Arrernte site and estate names were well-known to the present-day community, making clear and definitive object-to-place associations was not without difficulties. First, the descriptions for most objects contained references to multiple places; therefore, deciding upon a *primary* or *main* site association was often challenging. Should this be, for example, the place where a Dreaming narrative begins or ends, or somewhere else? As an example, the iconography on one wooden object was explained by Cowle as representing a story involving ancestors from the site of 'Nappeeper', a place located on the Burt Plain. While this place was quickly identified by Angeles and Inkamala as Anapipe (a large traditional landholding region to the north of Alice Springs), the documentation revealed that the ancestors referred to on the object were also closely connected to Terra, a place to the west. These complexities made the prospect of finding a definitive traditional owner extremely difficult. Were the 'traditional owners' those people connected to Terra or Anapipe? Who would now decide the terms of repatriation? Should the object be returned to the families belonging to the Anapipe or Terra, or could it be held in common by all Arrernte people at a mutually agreed location? Where was the 'home' for this object?

Beyond the difficulties of interpreting this documentation, the social worlds of these places had also changed. In the years and decades after these objects had been collected, Arrernte's social and cultural worlds continued to be severely disrupted. Settlers made slow but steady incursions into the region and episodes of violence and exploitation put people under considerable pressure (Austin-Broos 2009; Nettelbeck & Foster 2007). The social processes for inheriting and sharing religious objects and knowledge were also progressively undermined by these disruptions and exacerbated by the large-scale collection of sacred objects throughout the late nineteenth and early twentieth centuries (Jones 1995). Finding a home for these objects in the twenty-first century now involves much more than rediscovering their historical relationship to a place or set of places. As much as 'country' works to anchor collective and personal identities, returned objects also need to fit within living social and cultural realities. Where object documentation reveals complex and/or ill-defined relationships to place this reintegration is increasingly difficult. However, as the following case studies reveal, even where these relationships are more clearly described, putting objects back in place can remain troubling.

## Failed Homecomings

The intention of our mapping exercise was to identify objects that could ultimately be repatriated to their contemporary owners based on cultural relationships to place. Among the Cowle collection were 13 objects, including ten boomerangs, relating to the site of 'Mun-ung-unna' (Manangananga), a well-known sacred site to Western Arrernte people and often referred to in the history of the nearby Hermannsburg Mission. Situated downstream from the mission on the Finke River, Manangananga had once been home to sacred Arrernte objects but was openly de-sanctified by the missionaries and their Arrernte converts in 1928. The Hermannsburg Mission Pastor, F. W. Albrecht, and his Arrernte evangelists devised a picnic at nearby Manangananga, where psalms were sung and sermons recited. Manangananga was an important local repository of sacred objects, and its hoard included sacred boards associated with the local *arathepe* (baby) Dreaming. The site's senior Arrernte custodian, Titus Rengkareka, was among the evangelists who used Manangananga as the theatre to transgress the taboo associated with the exposure of these objects to the uninitiated (Jones 2007, pp. 331–332). The objects stored at Manangananga were removed, and women and children who would normally have been banished from the sacred area were invited to attend a picnic at the cave's entrance. The impact of this de-sanctification is still felt by members of the Hermannsburg community today, who, although able to happily reconcile both Christian and traditional Arrernte beliefs, acknowledge the attenuation of their traditional knowledge and practices (Batty 2014, pp. 297–298).

Rediscovering some of the Manangananga objects in the Cowle collection illuminates a much deeper and earlier history of collecting and trade. Thought to have been collected by the Lutheran missionaries and sold to German museums in the twentieth century, the cache of sacred boomerangs once kept at Manangananga was presumed to have been destroyed during the allied bombing raids of the Second World War (Strehlow 1971, p. 261). The Lutheran mission's close ties to Germany meant that they played a pivotal role in selling approximately 1,500 sacred objects to museums across Germany and Europe.[1] Following the bombing raids, some German museums reported significant losses, and hundreds of sacred objects were destroyed. Finding a reference to these boomerangs in Cowle's notes was, therefore, a moment of great surprise and celebration among the Arrernte men as a cache of extremely significant objects, presumed lost during a global war, had suddenly been rediscovered. The eight boomerangs had been described by Cowle as representing the ribs

1 Anthropologist and University of Göttingen researcher Olaf Geerken estimates that approximately 1,000–1,500 Central Australian *tywerrenge* were sent to German museums alone, but there are likely to be more in museums in Switzerland, Austria, and possibly elsewhere (Personal Communication 13/07/2021).

of a lizard ancestor (*tekentyarre, Ctenophorus isolepis*), and he noted that, 'in the early days', they had been used in combat and featured marks representing 'the number of *men killed* by being struck with the sharp side' (emphasis added).[2] This information matched Strehlow's description of the objects given to him by elderly Arrernte men as possessing supernatural power and being used as 'slayers' or 'men-killers' (1971, p. 269). Learning the boomerangs survived was considered an important event for the Western Arrernte community, but initial discussions about returning them to their home and re-united with their owners proved to be far more problematic.

The Melbourne Museum, which had supported the research and sincerely wanted to see a repatriation outcome, encouraged further community consultations. However, the response from the Arrernte community was suspicious following a recent, problematic attempt to return another significant object to the same community. There was now little appetite to revisit these complicated issues again. The sacred object in question had been 'found' (ostensibly stolen) from its traditional storage site by a collector in 1930 and subsequently donated to the Melbourne Museum in the 1960s. The museum was first approached with a request from a community member to have the object repatriated following a protracted land claim process in the 1990s. In the Northern Territory of Australia, recognition of Aboriginal rights to land can only be formally acknowledged through *The Aboriginal Land Rights (Northern Territory) Act 1976*, and different members of the community had been at loggerheads over who should be legally recognised as the traditional owners. The dispute hampered the granting of land rights for close to two decades; although a legal solution was eventually achieved, with one side being granted legal rights over the competing group, animosities persisted.

The volatilities associated with these land claims also came to influence people's interest in cultural heritage, particularly the possession of objects associated with the country in question. It was believed by some that taking possession of related and important sacred objects could bolster their claims to land. This scenario is particularly pertinent in Central Australia where sacred objects have been noted by land commissioners as being 'very closely linked to ownership of land and sometimes likened to title deeds. Their production by one group . . . must carry significant weight' (Gray 1999, p. 132). Different groups, therefore, sought to assert their rights to the country through the revelation of such objects and became interested in having certain objects returned to their possession via museum repatriation processes.

In this case, the Melbourne Museum's curator carried out extensive research and continued to have discussions with all interested parties but stopped short of initiating any formal repatriation procedures. It was argued

2 Collection documentation for items X9921 and X9924 in the Cowle Collection, Museum Victoria.

that, if an agreement could not be reached within the community about who would care for the object, how could it be cared for? Who would determine its future? It needed to be asked – would sending it back to the community be a divisive act and irresponsible on the part of the museum? Individuals wanting the object returned continued to advocate for its repatriation and downplayed the potential for community dispute. Those opposed remained quiet. It was proposed by the most vocal advocates for the object's return that an interim solution be sought, whereby the object could return to the Museum of Central Australia and Strehlow Research Centre, and then be briefly taken to its place of origin for a single night. It was argued that this would allow the community to discuss its attitude to the repatriation, allow people to reconnect with the object, and, most importantly, allow the object to be 'charged up' and be re-enlivened by being reconnected with its place of origin.

With agreement among diverse community representatives to trial this experimentation in object return, preparations began. The museum devised a risk matrix analysis, commissioned the manufacture of a custom casing for the object's transport, and recruited several consultants, including myself and two Arrernte men, to assist with community consultations. When the object arrived in Alice Springs and was delivered to the Strehlow Research Centre, it was met with a subdued but significant ceremony. The argument that the object needed to be 'charged up' at its source, where it had been left in the *Altyerre* (Dreaming), was restated. This, it was claimed, would 'open up the country' and allow the place to be revived by the object's spiritual potency. In preparation for the return, the repatriation team was guided to several sites associated with the object's ancestral story and museum staff shared documentation on the object from various archival sources.

On the eve of the repatriation event, however, the process began to fall apart. At 10:30 am, a member of a rival family arrived at the Strehlow Centre voicing his concerns over the return. Stated that he wanted more time for community discussions, he was clearly anxious about the plans. Disagreements emerged among the repatriation team. Some perceived this person's early intervention as an expression of caution and the need to proceed with care, while others were worried that this experimental return could seed further community disquiet. A short time later, another community member appeared at the Strehlow Centre expressing similar concerns. Visibly frightened and unable to hide his apprehension, he claimed that the return would likely result in family feuds and an increase in the use of traditional sorcery and possibly even led to deaths. He then turned to the museum staff and reminded them that, while they 'might feel good about repatriating a sacred object', they did not need to live with the repercussions. If there were negative consequences, his community would have to live with them, not the museum staff.

Lively discussions about the imperatives of repatriation ensued but were cut short when it was revealed that a police presence was requested by some in the community. Those who requested the police were fearful that the vehicle carrying the object to its site might be confronted as it passed through the community. It was clear that the return of this object, even for a day, was going to cause considerable community distress. As a result, the return was called off. The attempt to develop a new and innovative method of return to the place, as a first step towards repatriation, had to be abandoned. Subsequently, all parties agreed that, even though the contentious object could not be returned, it ought to stay in Alice Springs rather than Melbourne, over 2,300 km away. At the time of writing, six years on, the object has been visited occasionally by people from this community, but, like many other sacred objects that are sent to Central Australia by metropolitan state museums, it sits in its customised casing awaiting resolutions to complex community negotiations and an eventual homecoming.

## Different Colonial Space–Time Zones

In detailing these Central Australian case studies, I have illustrated some of the experimentations undertaken by both museums and communities when trying to associate sacred objects to place. In both scenarios, community knowledge of place-object-Dreaming relationships persists; however, the gradual attenuation of cultural knowledge and disagreements over land tenure have affected these processes. Disagreements over how an object might be socially and geographically repositioned have had important repercussions on repatriation and return initiatives in Central Australia.

In other parts of Australia, however, where longer histories of colonisation have resulted in considerably more social disruption, the web of place-people-story object relations has been under greater stress. The colonisation of southeastern Australia during the mid-1800s resulted in the devastation of the Aboriginal populace through acts of violence, the transmission of disease, and the active destruction of people's lifeways, as well as distinct forms of cultural safeguarding and endurance (Boyce 2011; Gibson & Mullet 2020). Cultural heritage collections belonging to different 'colonial space–time zones' (Morphy 2020, p. 47) will, therefore, present their own particular place-object challenges. People living in regions more significantly impacted by colonisation than in Central Australia possess what Beckett refers to as a kind of 'spirituality' where 'the bush' is more generally identified with 'the old people'. Cultural revivals have, therefore, centred upon re-establishing connections to 'wounded spaces' (Rose 2004) that have been torn and fractured by colonial expansion. Although these types of revivals have been noted elsewhere (Gray 1978; Beckett 2012; Merlan 2014), the role of ethnographic collections in this process, particularly in rebuilding the nexus between people, place, and story, is less well documented.

Between 2017 and 2020, I was part of an interdisciplinary team of scholars, working to digitise and transcribe the papers of the influential Australian anthropologist A. W. Howitt, a key early anthropologist in southeastern

Australia, who had been active during the colonial period. At the heart of this project was a desire to make Howitt's rich written archive more accessible to relevant Aboriginal communities and the wider public. We worked closely with several Aboriginal communities and organisations that had an interest in Howitt's writings about their ancestors, such as the Gippsland Land and Waters Aboriginal Corporation, the Wurundjeri Council, and the Dieri Aboriginal Corporation. We also collaborated with each of the collecting institutions that held Howitt materials, namely, the State Library of Victoria, the St. Marks Theological College Library, and the Melbourne Museum. Our team enlisted volunteers and community members to transcribe as much of Howitt's manuscript archive as possible within the three-year timeframe of the project (Hendery & Gibson 2019). As Howitt had lived and worked primarily in Kūrnai country in the far east of Victoria, and because he made important recordings of Yuin people to the immediate north in New South Wales, his ethnographic detail from these two groups was particularly significant. It was with representatives from these two groups that I began to explore how place informed and shaped the return of archival materials from a different 'colonial space–time zone'.

Both the Kūrnai and Yuin communities have had a long interest in Howitt's collection. His research into their ceremonial practices, social organisation, and kinship had an important impact on the way non-Indigenous peoples understood them, and in recent years, his publications have been avidly read and interrogated by the Kūrnai and Yuin themselves. Since the mid-1990s, most of Howitt's material culture collection had also been loaned by the Melbourne Museum to the local Krowathunkooloong Keeping Place in the country town of Bairnsdale (Woodcock & Hudson 2022). These objects continue to feature in the keeping place displays and are deeply treasured by the local community. Howitt had been a local magistrate in the area and employed Kūrnai people on his nearby hops farm. As such, his legacy looms large within the community.

For the Yuin, however, Howitt had been but a fleeting visitor who very briefly observed a part of ceremonial lives and collected scraps of information pertaining to their language, beliefs, and social organisation. Yuin elders who had heard about Howitt from their fathers (Ted Thomas and Percy Mumbulla) apparently described him as a 'used car salesman' as he had exaggerated his cultural position among the Kurnai in order to gain access to their ceremonial knowledge.[3] To them, Howitt had come with an agenda to extract as much information as he could from their 'old people'. Historical evidence also suggests that this was the case (Mulvaney 1970). Despite these differences in how Howitt has been remembered, both communities recognised the need to reclaim his fieldnotes and harness them for cultural revival work. The

3 Personal Communication with Chris 'Snappy' Griffiths 12/04/2019.

importance of understanding the contents of the collection in relation to place was again reiterated but, this time, in terms of outlining and/or re-asserting person–place relationships. As I have written elsewhere about the use of Howitt's archive to relocate a significant ceremonial ground in Kūrnai country (Gibson & Mullet 2020), the following case study focuses on similar work with the Yuin.

Having met with members of the Yuin community at Wallaga Lake in the autumn of 2019, a project was instigated to collaboratively interrogate Howitt's archive to find the site where, in 1883, he had witnessed a Kuringal – an abbreviated initiation ceremony for young men. A film detailing these investigations, including my own role in the process and re-enactments of Yuin song and dance performances by the Gulaga dancers, was later produced by the Yuin community (Cohen 2022). The production highlighted how Howitt's descriptions and sketches of the ceremonial ground had been important to re-think the significance of local cultural sites. The nearby Mumbulla Mountain, a place that had been protected from deforestation by Yuin elders in the 1980s due to its association with men's initiation rites (Egloff 1979), was generally believed to be the place where men had taken Howitt in 1883. Howitt's archive indicated otherwise. Howitt's notes and journalistic accounts from the time described the ceremonial site's proximity to the Bega township area as to the northeast in a secluded location of 'hilly country on the northern side of the Bega River not far from the sea coast'.[4] In a letter to R. H. Mathews, Howitt further described the location as 'in the hills about 5 miles easterly from the junction of the Bega and Brogo Rivers' (Mathews 1896, p. 316). He also noted that a creek nearby to the ceremonial ground ran into Nelson Lagoon. In reviewing this information and consulting maps, it was, therefore, agreed that the most likely site for the 1883 Kuringal would have been on Dr. George Mountain and not Mumbulla Mountain as had been assumed. A conclusion was also reached by Howitt's granddaughter (in Egloff 1979, p. 55) who claimed that the ceremony was 'probably on Dr. George Mountain near Bega'.

Over an 18-month period, Yuin men, including Warren Foster, Daniel Morgan, and Graeme Morris, led a research project to rediscover the place where the ceremony was held. They drew upon local knowledge of country and Howitt's archive, which included the names of the men who attended the ceremony. This information enabled us to draw direct familial links between the generations and brought the events of 1883 closer to the present generations. Among the attendees listed by Howitt were Peter Thomas and his son – the father and grandfather of the prominent Yuin activist of the later twentieth century, Ted Thomas. Johnny or Jack Mumbulla – also referred

4 See page 4 of Howitt MS 69, 7/2/1, a handwritten draft manuscript titled *Kuringal*.

to as 'King Biamanga' and the father of the equally well-known Yuin poet, storyteller, and leader Percy Mumbulla – was also noted as being present.[5] Close to 40 other men were listed in Howitt's notebook, and many of their contemporary descendants were also identified. Making these intergenerational connections was significant for bringing the historical into the present, but it was the work of relocating the site of the Kuringal and traversing the landscape with copies of Howitt's archival materials in hand, which engendered considerable interest.

Working through Howitt's collection *in situ* gave rise to a different kind of understanding; one where the sense of temporal distance is suspended, and a co-presence across time and space (with 'old people') is evoked. As one community researcher commented:

> We think about our collections research as a way of as visiting the 'old people' as much as 'place'. I know it sounds fuzzy, but that sense of time collapsing, even briefly, is meaningful to understanding place and history. It's indispensable. Being able to locate place and connect people and objects in history to people in the present day; that is really closing the circle – we try to do that through our collections research, in our own way.[6]

One of the challenges of this work, however, was the changed nature of the landscape itself. In the intervening 140 years since the Kuringal had been documented, forestry and pastoralism had altered the countryside, and in some places, the ground itself had been reshaped by the fervent digging of gold miners throughout the late nineteenth and early twentieth centuries. The land tenure of the place had also been transformed. Yuin lands had been parcelled up into private property, nature reserves, and national parks. Re-finding the ceremonial site was, therefore, a significant challenge.

In this case, while the specific site of the Kuringal remained elusive to the team, the historical and fieldwork methods used by the community became critical to finding new value in the archive. The interaction between social memory, orality, collections, and archives afforded new opportunities for knowing country. As one community participant commented:

> Going to the historical record to find ceremonial sites, important campsites, burial places, etc, re-locating them initially on maps, and then in the field, based on evidence, it can be done . . . and it has so much potential meaning . . . to fill in the gaps in oral historical knowledge. Some people don't like this kind of learning from books and collections and see it as overriding 'traditional knowledge', but plenty of people are really open to

5 A.W. Howitt Collection, Museum Victoria, XM761 field notebook.

6 Personal Communication with J. Durant 4/08/2020.

> it and are very interested. If we find something we think is significant – an object, a map, an entry in an old field book or letter – the first thing we do is share it with appropriate elders. It is exciting. We're excited and we want to tell someone who cares. We want to keep working in this mode. Hopefully this can help people reconnect with place in country, which was really impacted since very early on.

## Conclusion

This chapter analysed how different Aboriginal people and groups in Australia are grappling with the task of reconnecting returned museum collections and archives to place. The examples from Central Australia demonstrate the particularistic nature of these reconnections and how complex and fraught returns to the country can be. In this cultural context, individuals and family groups with religious connections to certain places (either through inheritance or spiritual conception) are required to take responsibility for objects of high cultural and religious value. However, due to the attenuated and disrupted nature of people's relationships to land, the work of reconnection is far from simple.

Detailed collection documentation, especially particulars relating to Dreamings and specific sites, has become prized information among these communities. When given the opportunity, communities will eagerly work with collecting institutions to search for evidence pertaining to ancestral stories and place names that might help re-emplace objects. This has become a hugely important grounding activity. It invites communities to bring their associated social and cultural knowledge to the fore, build bridges between past and present, actively interrogate catalogue and associated collection documentation, and work with interested researchers in object mapping and experiment with emergent repatriation practices.

Objects re-enter changed and changing landscapes. These places have been transformed by the disruptive ecological and social transformations of settler-colonialism, changed cultural practices, and introduced forms of land tenure and legal frameworks. Disputes over land, such as those discussed in this chapter, are likely to continue affecting repatriation endeavours and other cultural heritage claims into the future. This settler-colonial reality now sees objects being used in new ways. The *tywerrenge* of Central Australia is, for example, not only regarded as objects of religious veneration within Aboriginal society but also seen as 'evidence' of traditional ownership in Australian legal settings. In southeast Australia, where more fine-grained associations have been more-deeply attenuated, the meaning of archival and museum objects nevertheless also continues to be found in place. The Howitt archive, for example, was used not just to attempt a relocation of specific sites but to reinvigorate connections to places in general. The return of these objects, thus, served as a catalyst not only to journey through Yuin country but also to re-situate historical material. The emplacement of these archives, thus, came about through an active engagement with the past in the present, a set of actions that moved the object beyond the merely evidential towards the affective. Working through Howitt's collection *in situ* also gave rise to a different kind of understanding where the sense of temporal distance was suspended and a co-presence across time and space was evoked. This is not a miraculous process or a return to a pre-colonial appreciation of place but a contemporary practice, whereby archives and museum collections may help to generate a cultural future.

## References

Anderson, C. 1995, *Politics of the Secret,* Oceania Monographs 45, University of Sydney, Sydney.

Austin-Broos, D. 2009, *Arrernte Present, Arrernte Past: Invasion, Violence, and Imagination in Indigenous Central Australia*, University of Chicago Press, Chicago.

Batty, P. 2014, 'The Tywerrenge as an Artefact of Rule: The (Post) Colonial Life of a Secret/Sacred Aboriginal Object', *History and Anthropology,* vol. 25, no. 2, pp. 296–311, https://doi.org/10.1080/02757206.2014.882833.

Beckett, J. 2012, 'Returned to Sender: Some Predicaments of Re-Indigenisation', *Oceania,* vol. 82, no. 1, pp. 104–112, https://doi.org/10.1002/j.1834-4461.2012.tb00122.x.

Boyce, J. 2011, *1835: The Founding of Melbourne and the Conquest of Australia*, Black Inc, Collingwood, Victoria.

Carty, J. 2019, 'To Imagine an Australian Museum', *Anthropological Forum,* vol. 29, no. 4, pp. 384–396, https://doi.org/10.1080/00664677.2019.1706038.

Carty, J. 2021, *Balgo: Creating Country*, UWA Publishing, Perth.

Casey, E.S. 1996, 'How to Get from Space to Place in a Fairly Short Stretch of Time: Phenomenological Prolegomena', in S. Feld & K. Basso (eds), *Senses of Place: School of American Research Advanced Seminar Series*, 1st ed., School of American Research Press, Santa Fe, pp. 13–52.

Cohen, S, dir. 2022, *Kuringal*, Canberra, accessed from https://vimeo.com/669641373.

DoCA. 2019, *Fact Sheet: Indigenous Repatriation – International*, Department of Communication and the Arts, Australian Government, Canberra.

Egloff, B. 1979, *Mumbulla Mountain: An Anthropological and Archealogical Investigation*, National Parks and Wildlife Service, NSW, Sydney.

Gibson, J. & Mullet, R. 2020, 'The Last Jeraeil of Gippsland: Rediscovering an Aboriginal Ceremonial Site', *Ethnohistory,* vol. 67, no. 4, pp. 551–577, https://doi.org/10.1215/00141801-8579216.

Gray, D. 1978, 'A Revival of the Law: The Probable Spread of Initiation Circumcision to the Coast of Western Australia', *Oceania,* vol. 48, no. 3, pp. 188–201.

Gray, P. 1999, *Palm Valley Land Claim. 48*, Report no. 57, Aboriginal and Torres Strait Islander Commission, Canberra, accessed from www.dss.gov.au/sites/default/files/documents/05_2012/57.pdf.

Harvey, M. 2002, 'Land Tenure and Naming Systems in Aboriginal Australia', *The Australian Journal of Anthropology,* vol. 13, no. 1, pp. 23–44, https://doi.org/10.1111/j.1835-9310.2002.tb00188.x.

Hendery, R. & Gibson, J. 2019, 'Crowdsourcing Downunder', *KULA: Knowledge Creation, Dissemination, and Preservation Studies,* vol. 3, no. 1, pp. 1–12, https://doi.org/10.5334/kula.52.

Hercus, L., Hodges, F. & Simpson, J. (eds). 2002, *The Land Is a Map: Placenames of Indigenous Origin in Australia,* Pandanus Books, Research School of Pacific and Asian Studies, The Australian National University, Canberra.

Jones, P.G. 1995, '"Objects of Mystery and Concealment": A History of Tjurunga Collecting', in C. Anderson (ed), *Politics of the Secret,* Oceania Monograph 45, University of Sydney, Sydney, pp. 67–96.

Jones, P.G. 2007, *Ochre and Rust: Artefacts and Encounters on Australian Frontiers,* Wakefield Press, Adelaide.

Kean, J. 2023, *Art of the Dot, Circle and Frame, How Kaapa Tjampitjinpa, Tim Leura Tjapaltjarri and Johnny Warangula Tjupurrula Invented Contemporary Desert Art,* Upswell, Perth.

Keen, I. 1997, 'The Western Desert vs the Rest: Rethinking the Contrast', in F. Merlan, J. Morton, & A. Rumsey (eds), *Scholar and Sceptic,* Aboriginal Studies Press, Canberra, pp. 65–94.

Mathews, R.H. 1896, 'The Burbung of the Wiradthuri Tribes', *The Journal of the Anthropological Institute of Great Britain and Ireland,* vol. 25, pp. 295–318, https://doi.org/10.2307/2842029.

Merlan, F. 2014, 'Recent Rituals of Indigenous Recognition in Australia: Welcome to Country', *American Anthropologist,* vol. 116, no. 2, pp. 296–309, https://doi.org/10.1111/aman.12089.

Morphy, H. 2020, *Museums, Infinity and the Culture of Protocols: Ethnographic Collections and Source Communities,* Routledge, London.

Mulvaney, D.J. 1970, 'The Anthropologist as Tribal Elder', *Mankind,* vol. 7, no. 3, pp. 205–217, https://doi.org/10.1111/j.1835-9310.1970.tb00409.x.

Mulvaney, D.J., Petch, A. & Morphy, H. 2000, *From the Frontier: Outback Letters to Baldwin Spencer,* Allen & Unwin, St. Leonards, NSW.

Nettelbeck, A. & Foster, R. 2007, *In the Name of the Law: William Willshire and the Policing of the Australian Frontier,* Wakefield Press, Adelaide.

Peterson, N. & Long, J. 1986, *Australian Territorial Organization: A Band Perspective,* vol. 30, Oceania Monograph, University of Sydney, Sydney.

Phillips, R.B. 2005, 'Re-Placing Objects: Historical Practices for the Second Museum Age', *The Canadian Historical Review,* vol. 86, no. 1, pp. 83–110, https://doi.org/10.1353/can.2005.0086.

Pickering, M. 2015, '"The Big Picture": The Repatriation of Australian Indigenous Sacred Objects', *Museum Management and Curatorship,* vol. 30, no. 5, pp. 427–443, https://doi.org/10.1080/09647775.2015.1054418.

Porr, M. 2018, 'Country and Relational Ontology in the Kimberley, Northwest Australia: Implications for Understanding and Representing Archaeological Evidence', *Cambridge Archaeological Journal,* vol. 28, no. 3, pp. 395–409, https://doi.org/10.1017/S0959774318000185.

Rose, D.B. 2004, *Reports from a Wild Country: Ethics for Decolonisation,* UNSW Press, Sydney.

Sansom, B. 2006, 'The Brief Reach of History and the Limitation of Recall in Traditional Aboriginal Societies and Cultures', *Oceania,* vol. 76, no. 2, pp. 150–172.

Sculthorpe, G. 2019, 'Provenance and Place in Indigenous Australia', in J. Pearce & N. Milosch (eds), *Collecting and Provenance: A Multidisciplinary Approach*, Rowman & Littlefield Publishing Group, Lanham, Maryland, pp. 269–279.

Strehlow, T.G.H. 1971, *Songs of Central Australia*, Angus and Robertson, Sydney.

Sutton, P. 1995, *Country: Aboriginal Boundaries and Land Ownership in Australia*, ACT: Aboriginal History, Canberra.

Tilley, C. 2004, *Materiality of Stone: Explorations in Landscape Phenomenology*, Bloomsbury Publishing, London, UK, accessed from http://ebookcentral.proquest.com/lib/deakin/detail.action?docID=243525.

Turner, H. 2020, *Cataloguing Culture Legacies of Colonialism in Museum Documentation*, University of British Columbia Press, Vancouver.

Turner, M.K. 2010, *Iwenhe Tyerrtye: What It Means to Be an Aboriginal Person*, V. Dobson (trans), IAD Press, Alice Springs.

Woodcock, S. & Hudson, R. 2022, *Self-Determined First Nations Museums and Colonial Contestation: The Keeping Place*, Routledge, London.

# 4 Digital Returns of Anmatyerr Ceremonial Performance and New Collecting

Mr. Michael Tommy is one of the many Aboriginal elders across Australia, who has been sounding the alarm on Indigenous performance traditions for decades. 'We are the second last generation. If these younger men do not follow us, it is all finished. Our songs and ceremonies will die out in five to ten years'.[1] These concerns are by no means exaggerated. The musicologist Allan Marett has, for example, concluded the classical performance traditions that

> survive today, mainly in the remote northern and central parts of Australia, represents only a tiny fraction of what was, at the time of first European contact, a vast, rich and dynamic ceremonial complex that reached into every corner of the continent.

Marett goes on to state, in terms very similar to Mr. Tommy, that even these remaining traditions are so critically endangered that they are unlikely to 'survive for more than another generation or two' (Marett 2010, p. 253).

Such gloomy predictions have been reinforced in recent statements from the International Council for Traditional Music that now estimates that approximately 98% of Indigenous Australian musical traditions, which are usually accompanied by a dance performance, have been lost. It is under this spectre of loss that audio–visual recordings of performances have begun to re-enter Indigenous communities from the museum and archival collections. Aimed at stemming this downward trajectory but also providing people with rightful access to their cultural inheritance, initiatives to return recordings of songs and ceremonies have increased in recent decades, both in Australia (Treloyn, Martin & Charles 2016; Bracknell 2019; Campbell 2014) and abroad (Gunderson, Lancefield & Woods 2018; Hilder 2012). It is often implied that the return of archival recordings will play a role in seeing defunct traditions

1 Personal Communication with M. Tommy at Laramba 14/09/2022.

DOI: 10.4324/9781003158752-4

revived or threatened ones maintained. This chapter will interrogate that claim though the recirculation of films and audio recordings of male ceremonial performances of the Anmatyerr communities.

This chapter examines a decade-long process of returning film and audio recordings of ceremonial performances made by the anthropologist and linguist T. G. H. Strehlow to Anmatyerr communities between 2012 and 2022. Working in partnership with numerous Anmatyerr song and ceremonial experts, including Mr. Tommy and over 40 other men from across the region, these recordings were returned in various digital formats and often in conjunction with other related collection documentation, such as song transcriptions and translations, as well as relevant field diary entries.

The continued relevance of these religious ceremonial performances, as well as the place of song in everyday life, made the return of these recordings a matter of great interest, as people experimented with different ways that they might utilise recordings in contemporary life. The literature on the return of archival song recordings to Indigenous communities is growing; however, there has been little ethnographic work on how copies have been managed and utilised after an initial handover. Contributing to this field of study, this chapter attempts to go beyond the apparent moral benefits of access and gain insight into the complex resonances of these collections beyond acts of cultural maintenance or revival. As is revealed later, the return of Strehlow's ritually charged material has been a complex process, and the outcomes of this return have been determined as much by the contingencies of life in remote Indigenous communities as by the expertise and intentions of the agents of return (collecting institution and researchers). While I have entered into dialogue with Anmatyerr people to better understand the histories of these collections (Gibson 2020), the purpose of this chapter is to fathom the complexities of these recordings in the present and how they figure in peoples' relations with others.

In Anmatyerr communities where song and ceremonial traditions persist, the return of these archives has led to unanticipated consequences. Perhaps, one of the more surprising outcomes of these returns has been people's insistence that further recordings of song and ceremony can be made. Years of collaborative interrogation of the Strehlow audio–visual archive have led to what I have labelled 'new collecting' – a kind of collaborative, Indigenous-led collecting made in response to the return of older collections. Teasing out the reasons for these moves is critically important to think about the prospects of ethnographic collections as intercultural domains (Jonaitis & Glass 2010) and sites of collaboration (Peers & Brown 2003; Conway 2021; Wanambi, Skerritt & McDonald 2022). It adds new dimensions to the well-worn notion of the museum as a 'contact zone' (Clifford 1997). While the benefits of collaborations in Indigenous exhibition development are now well-understood (Peers & Brown 2003; Phillips 2003), less has been written about Indigenous groups creating and offering new objects and collections to pair with historical collections.

Some examples of this new collecting are, nonetheless, emerging. Menang people in South West Western Australia have, in recent years, gained access to an early ichthyology collection made in 1839 and now held at the National Museums of Scotland that contains detailed Indigenous knowledge recorded from their ancestors (Smith 2022). In response, the Menang people have instigated a new partnership with the museum to catch, preserve, and document fish in a way that honours the depth of Menang knowledge but also directly responds to and augments the 1839 collection.[2] In the case study provided later, I suggest that the invitation to participate in new collecting could only ever follow years of careful engagement. The preconditions for such a partnership would, therefore, need to include improved and ongoing access to collections, sensitive collaborations that recognise Indigenous rights, the elevation of Indigenous epistemologies, and building awareness and an acknowledgement of the historical agency of Anmatyerr people in the making of the collection.

The return of these recordings has instigated a desire among people to reiterate and reinstate their contemporary, tacit, and explicit ceremonial knowledge in a changed yet related form. These moves, I came to appreciate, made the point that these historical recordings of ceremonial performances could only ever be understood in response to peoples' changing social contexts and in a dialectical interplay with the present. In the context of Anmatyerr society, where classical song and performance repertoires are vulnerable but persist, these recordings were regarded as historically and culturally significant, yet their return was principally valued for what they might add to present practice and in the building of new relationships.

## Strehlow's Audio–Visual Archive

Between 1932 and 1974, the anthropologist and linguist T. G. H. Strehlow assembled what has since been described as 'the most complete collection of cultural material of any First People in Australia and possibly the world' (Perkins 2016). As a student of the classics and languages, Strehlow's initial focus had been on the transcription and translation of Central Australian Aboriginal song texts and mythologies that he then augmented with opportunistic collecting of related artefacts. The interrelations between mythology, song, and ceremonial performance in this part of Australia, and their foundations in a land-based religion, meant that Strehlow soon found himself embroiled in an effort to create a comprehensive record of Arrernte traditions (Strehlow 1947). Relying initially upon carefully handwritten transcriptions of people's songs and stories using his own orthography for the Arandic languages (Arrernte and Anmatyerr), by the 1950s, he had embraced innovations in audio–visual

2 Personal Communication with Tiffany Shellam 2/12/2022.

technology to capture song and dance performances. With the intent of refuting erroneous, colonial assumptions that Aboriginal songs were mere vocalisations absent of meaning, Strehlow used his recordings, transcriptions, and English translations to document their complexity, beauty, and significance. His magnum opus, *Songs of Central Australia* (1971), is recognised as one of the most significant testaments to an Aboriginal song ever published despite its limitations (see Jorgensen 2010; Gibson 2020, pp. 88–90). Closely related to this recording of the song, however, was the documentation of ceremonial performances on colour film between 1950 and 1971. Given strict gender domains between male and female religious and ceremonial knowledge in Central Australia, Strehlow worked only with men and recorded only male performances.

To properly understand the content and context of traditional songs, Strehlow learned very early on that he also needed to witness, and record, related ceremonial performances. The technological limitations of the times required that separate audio and film recordings can be made. As such, Strehlow would often film a ceremony and then later sit with the relevant performers in his caravan to make audio recordings of songs sung at different intervals of a ritual. After Strehlow's death in 1978, the collection was subject to numerous ownership disputes and repatriation requests from the Central Australian Aboriginal people, resulting in the establishment of the Strehlow Research Centre in 1991 – a custom-built facility in the township of Alice Springs with central proximity to the relevant Aboriginal communities. Since that time, Aboriginal men and women have progressively achieved greater access to the collection and the distribution of copies of the manuscript, and audio–visual materials are closely managed by an Arrernte collections researcher and the Strehlow Research Centre Board (led by local Aboriginal membership). In 2012, I began working with the Strehlow Research Centre to return many of these filmic and audio recordings to identified senior cultural experts across Anmatyerr communities. As I began to reassess Strehlow's audio–visual collection, I wanted to know, among other things, the degree to which people possessed the requisite cultural knowledge to interpret and relate to the songs and ceremonies that Strehlow had recorded. What did contemporary people still know about them?

Before launching into my collaborative explorations of this archive with the Anmatyerr people though, it was critical to interrogate the history behind the assembly of this material. Born to Carl and Frieda Strehlow, Lutheran missionaries at the remote Hermannsburg mission in 1908, young Theodor George Heinrich (T. G. H.) Strehlow had been raised among speakers of the Aboriginal languages Arrernte and Luritja but also learned German and English. His parents had immigrated to Australia as missionaries from Germany in the late nineteenth century and had devoted themselves to learning the language of the Aboriginal people they encountered to aide them in their missionising efforts. Young Strehlow, therefore, grew up speaking Arrernte and came to possess knowledge of, and an appreciation for, Arrernte cultural lives. His father, Carl Strehlow, was an excellent ethnographer in his own right and had devoted considerable time transcribing traditional songs and ancestral stories (Kenny 2013). In the shadow of his father, T. G. H. Strehlow went on to accrue over 150 hours of song recordings, film hundreds of ceremonial performances, and create maps of sacred totemic sites that covered much of Central Australia.

As a collector and recordist, Strehlow exhibited considerable hubris. Not only did he believe that he alone had come to possess any depth of Arandic ceremonial knowledge but also he failed to comprehend the adaptations, negotiations, and strategies that people had applied to cultural practice in the face of colonial disruption (Hill 2003). His attitude is exemplified in this field diary entry from 1965 following the recording of performances and collection of objects associated with the Anmatyerr site of Korbula:

> [N]o one else will ever again be allowed to make another final Korbula ground painting, sing its songs, or use again the designs done on its two alkuta [shields] unless I authorise such a thing . . . these are all my personal property from now on.
>
> (Strehlow 1965, p. 48)

Returning these collections to contemporary Anmatyerr and Arrernte communities has, therefore, been a project of cultural restoration and acknowledgement of people's cultural rights.

## Collaborative Returns

When I began to return copies of selected audio–visual recordings to Anmatyerr communities in 2012, I was initially struck by how much of this material was still known to people. Not only did the men that I presented these recordings to easily identify and sing along with many of the song recordings but also they explained the significance of most ceremonies and were able to reconnect this material to known sacred sites. Admittedly, these were often older men aged between 60 and 90 years, but many younger men had also been instructed in at least the rudiments of these traditions. It was clear that, just as Strehlow had failed to appreciate how these performances were being taught and circulated among Central Australian men, others since had uncritically adopted this linear narrative of cultural decline (Smith 2009, pp. 85–86) and failed to appreciate a more complex picture. There was evidently a more nuanced interplay between the complexities of loss, continuity, and change at work here, and ethnographic research was required to see how these ritually charged recordings might be returned to communities that had to deal with competing expectations of tradition and change.

Developing a method for the return of Strehlow's recordings emerged after many years of discussions with the Anmatyerr and Arrernte people. Different men approached me over the years asking for more information on the contents of the Strehlow collection and how they might access this material. Over a decade, I was able to play back these films and audio recordings to over 60 different men living in the Anmatyerr communities of Nthwerrey, Ti Tree, Six Mile, Alyuen, Laramba, Engawala, Mulga Bore, and Ahalper, as well as in the township of Alice Springs. As people listened to and watched recordings, their insightful commentary and responses conveyed much about the value of ceremonial performance but also 'cultural endangerment' (Jackson 2007). As I was not concerned with translating these performances or assessing their greater anthropological significance, my focus was on the affordances of these recordings and understanding what existential impacts their return might have.

Only two of the performers who had danced and sung for Strehlow's cameras in the late 1960s were still alive. Though both remembered their encounters with Strehlow, neither never had the opportunity to hear the recordings of their voices and see their performances on film. Other men recognised their fathers and/or grandfathers and used the return of these materials to educate younger generations about the historical context in which these recordings were made. It was noted that these recordings had been made when Aboriginal people undoubtedly had fewer rights but at the same time they wanted the agency, vision, and foresight of these performers in the making of this collection to be acknowledged. Anmatyerr elder Teddy Briscoe Mpetyan, for example, recalled that, when he was a young man working on cattle stations to the north of Alice Springs in the 1950s, he had been told about these recording and collecting events by one of Strehlow's key collaborators, the Arrernte elder Bob Rubuntja. Rubuntja had apparently expressed regret that the young Teddy had 'missed out' on being involved in Strehlow's recordings work in Alice Springs and urged him to be involved if the opportunity arose again.

So eager were people to engage with these recordings, I was usually told to start playback immediately. Having already been through an exhaustive process of archival research to identify appropriate Anmatyerr song recordings, upon arrival, I was usually well-prepared to present selected materials. The tremendous interest in the song collection meant that those with close personal associations with the material, or who were regarded as expert singers, would soon be gathered in anticipation. Being aware of the political issues that can also arise regarding disputed ownership and control over sites, ceremonies, and songs, I was ever mindful of choosing the 'right' content to discuss with the 'right' people. In accordance with the general principles of the Central Australian knowledge economy (Pink 1936; Michaels 1985), this meant ensuring that the owners (*merek-artwey*) or managers (*kwertengerl*) for different performances were present during playback. The cultural, gender, and age restrictions placed on this material also meant that the group listening sessions would often transpire at a location far away from women and children.

Located away from general daily comings and goings in the community, the participants were free to listen to recordings or watch films without being overheard by women or children.

At the conclusion of numerous collaborative listening and viewing sessions, Anmatyerr men were often provided with digital copies of selected recordings. These were given either to the men who featured in them, their immediate kin, or others who were recognised as possessing significant cultural expertise. Decisions about how the materials would be used, stored, and distributed were left entirely up to the men. Returns of this type had been tentatively trialled over a decade earlier with analogue copies reportedly being 'buried' in caves for safe keeping (Hersey & Cohen 2004, p. 183). Since 2012, I have been also witnessing CDs, DVDs, and, more recently, USBs, being stored alongside sacred objects that had been repatriated in recent decades from various Australian museums. People also share these recordings among their relations but often struggle to find suitable devices to play older formats. Limited technological infrastructure and resources in these impoverished communities make the storage and management of this material in the long-term extremely problematic. While it is acknowledged that the return of digital copies provides an unreliable and short-term solution, it remains the best way of providing access and raising awareness about the collection among Anmatyerr stakeholders. Copies circulate for a period and raise interest, but formats suffer from inoperability issues, and copies are either lost or damaged. Without a central repository, such as a local museum, keeping place, or archive, the replenishing of copies tends to rely upon interested researchers acting as a bridge between communities and the Strehlow Research Centre.

## Re-integrating Recordings

Being an active participant in these return processes for over a decade, I have endeavoured to keep an ethnographic account of how these recordings have been re-integrated. Often after providing people with copies, men would later approach me wanting to perform their knowledge of these traditions. On one such occasion in 2016, a middle-aged man from the Coniston area, who I had not seen for several years, approached me at the local roadhouse wanting to discuss these issues. He had been out most of the day working on a nearby cattle station and was rounding the day off with a beer. In this unlikely place, he wanted to talk about Strehlow's recordings and spoke about an ancestral *pelyakw* (duck) that had travelled through his own country before singing a snippet of its song. He described the bird's peregrinations as it moved between several sites and named some of the senior men who had taught him these things.

As much as my work in these communities had established frank personal connections, I also understood that both he and I occupied a range of positions in relation to each other. This work had situated me as someone whose place was to show interest in Anmatyerr traditions, help locate and retrieve further collections of interest, and attempt resource-related activities. Men like him, in return, would repay me for these undertakings by sharing information, knowledge, and experiences distinctive to Anmatyerr 'traditional culture' that, I, as a museum anthropologist, presumably valued. These relationships also had historical precedent as the symbolic labour of ceremonial performance and trade in traditional artefacts had become an acknowledged currency between non-Indigenous people and Central Australians for over a century.

The recitation of songs and the performance of rituals in Anmatyerr society continue to be a feature of everyday life. These performances are used not only in religious contexts but also to heal the sick, control the weather, honour ancestors, record social histories, and attract lovers (Turpin 2014; Duwell & Dixon 1994). The recordings made by Strehlow, however, almost exclusively prioritised male religious ceremonies pertaining to different local estates. As many of these ceremonies continue to be enacted during annual initiation events, many of Strehlow's recordings were immediately familiar. In scenarios like this, where people have managed to braid pre-colonial traditions together with adaptions to coloniality, there is less urgency to give these recordings 'back' as anthropologist Barbara Glowczewski has written (2020, p. 287). Instead, Anmatyerr people often expressed an interest in providing collecting institutions with important information about the cultural context and value of the material that they held. Having had copies of some of these recordings for several years now, elders have not asked for the recordings to be returned but for their status as cultural rights holders and experts on the performance content to be properly recognised. Accepting that collecting institutions would hold these recordings into the future, Anmatyerr people wanted their expert counsel to guide its future uses.

Possessing digital copies of these recordings can also produce a degree of anxiety about their distribution. Though the Strehlow Research Centre was comfortable in providing digital copies to the relevant cultural experts, the community still needed to find locally acceptable solutions for safe storage and distribution. As these performances are treated with extreme sensitivity and thought precious or 'dear', access to them would usually only occur in the context of dialogue and interaction with elders and via the making ceremonial payments known as *tyewarrely*. Any contravention of the protocols could be costly, both in terms of local reputation, but men also speak of threats of physical harm if these traditions are broken. The arrival of these recordings can, therefore, unsettle social relationships by offering younger men, in particular, an enticing opportunity to learn traditions via the archive, rather than instruction from elders. In one of the few ethnographic studies of how repatriated collections are managed in a source community, Lissant Bolton has pointed to the status of those individuals that involve themselves in this cultural heritage work in the Erromangan communities of Vanuatu. 'In becoming the repositories of so much knowledge', these individuals establish 'themselves as powerfully knowledgeable in a society that has always greatly valued knowledge as a resource' (Bolton 2015, p. 245). At the same time, they work to provide a foundation for Indigenous identity that is based on the knowledge and practice of the past. Contemporary knowledge holders may, therefore, feel inadequate, challenged, or even threatened as the voices and actions of their ancestors come back – in mediated form – half a century later to unsettle the present.

This phenomenon was most evident following the return of recordings of ceremonial performances or songs that are now less well-known or not known at all. Don Pengart's reactions to having copies of Strehlow's recording of the *anterrng artety* (mulga seed) verses from Angenty encapsulate this tension perfectly. Obviously being excited to hear a song to which he belonged, Don could not, however, disguise his melancholy. Segments of the song were clearly familiar enough for him to sing along with the recording, but, having witnessed the far more active ceremonial life 'back in the 1970s' when it had 'still been working', he lamented that, now, it was now 'all gone'. Elder Ronnie McNamara, too, despite personally possessing an expansive knowledge of these songs and traditions, claimed that the frequency and significance of ceremonial activity for the Anmatyerr had certainly diminished. Some of the songs that Strehlow had recorded with men who were Ronnie's classificatory fathers were apparently unknown to men today. After listening to these recordings, Ronnie responded with great emotion and fragility in his voice. He looked to the ground and shook his head in disbelief. 'That's the first time'. His voice trailed off. A few other men, also bemused and saddened that they missed out on learning these songs, whispered *lyetant awem*, 'the first time I've heard this'. Attention would then shift to the songs and ceremonies still known, and it was copies of these performances alone, which were requested for community use.

These responses are included here not to suggest that the recordings are of no value to contemporary Anmatyerr communities. On the contrary, they possess considerable power. What is demonstrated here is that their return has not led to the type of cultural revival this kind of return is often assumed to automatically produce. As observed by the North American anthropologist Tamara Bray (1996, p. 442), the idea that the return of collections will automatically lead to maintenance or revival of cultural practices is ultimately a 'misguided' one as cultural identity does not reside in either artefacts or recordings. Furthermore, the preservation of these materials is often not a high priority for marginalised groups who focus on their own becoming and emphasise capacities to endure and transform the worlds they inhabit rather than endlessly duplicate the past. At least, in Anmatyerr communities, what has taken greater precedence is the upholding of practices that still have currency for people today, and this has led to an expressed desire to make further, new collections.

## New Collecting

It was very early in my returns of the Strehlow recordings that I was challenged by Anmatyerr men to instigate new recordings. Some asked me to *pwetewem-ilem*, 'take photos and films', as they re-enacted performances or recited songs, and I was regularly instructed to *ingkwernem-ilem*, 'put down in writing', people's elucidations. Others were more ambitious and advocated for a project called 'Strehlow Part Two' that would set out to record many of the same ceremonies with contemporary knowledge holders from across the region. People also understood that the contextual information that they provided to Strehlow's recordings – where someone was from, and their relationships to land, their kin, and so on – would make all the difference for future generations trying to make sense of the material. Though I did my best to record the details of people's responses and conduct good ethnography, I was reticent to become a 'collector'. Fearful of replicating collecting practices that might enable yet another white, non-Indigenous, male to accumulate materials belonging to Indigenous Australians, I dodged repeated invitations to take on a larger role in collecting. As the years went by, I was struck by how often these requests to make recordings like Strehlow's were repeated. I had to ask if it was my own 'white anti-racist' position, which fretted over an assumed 'inherent capacity to damage Indigenous people' (Kowal 2015, p. 25), which had caused me to disregard these requests from the Anmatyerr people.

There was little doubt that the return of Strehlow's audio–visual collections had directly, yet unintentionally, led to these proposals. Seeing and hearing their ancestor cooperating with Strehlow as he filmed and recorded their treasured cultural performances gave legitimacy to any contemporary interest in engaging in something similar. The invitations continued, and by 2021, nearly a decade after the first digital returns had occurred, I agreed to provide some assistance. Working with men from the community of Laramba, we co-designed the initiative *Anmatyerr shields, songs and ceremonies: a heritage project for community and Nation*. The project's intention was to document vulnerable ceremonial and artistic traditions, and support elders in their instruction to younger generations as they showed them how to produce unique shield designs and perform associated songs and dances. In his reasoning for the project, Martin Hagan Mpetyan cited the return of the Strehlow materials as its impetus:

> We have these old recordings, but we want to sit down again and record the songs that our old people know today. We can update the record. We can match it with Strehlow's . . . As the years go by, there aren't many Anmatyerr men who know these special songs. You need a group. A car needs four wheels. It can't drive on one or two wheels. As a younger man I have been involved in a lot of ceremonies and I see every year a decline of culture, particularly our designs and different songs and dances. If we lose

our old people, we lose these things. That's why it is important to record these songs, their body paint designs and stories as soon as possible.[3]

In the 14 support letters attached to the funding submission needed to resource this work, other Anmatyerr men made similar appeals. One man wrote that 'the recording and preservation of our ceremonies have been neglected in recent years, and there is now a real need to record as much as we can for future generations'. Another explained that 'the knowledge that we want to collect and record is what we call *anengkerr-iperre* [from the Dreaming] . . . support for this project will ensure that this knowledge is nurtured for future generations'. Elders in the community wrote a combined letter stating that 'it is important to preserve and keep our younger generation educated about Culture, The Law, and ways . . . The extensive knowledge that will be recorded and preserved will benefit generations to come'.[4] Grounded in the language of salvage, this project was able to garner resources to assist with the reproduction and re-enactment of a distinctive Anmatyerr identity. Numerous Anmatyerr songs and ceremonies, some identical to those recorded by Strehlow 60 years earlier, were performed, and decorated shields were produced as physical augmentations to the audio–visual record (Figure 4.1). The necessity of collecting in this way was reiterated by elder Michael Tommy who commented that, like Strehlow's collecting with older generations, it was important to take a wholistic approach. 'You can't just make the shield and give it. You have to perform the ceremony and sing the songs too. Then we can be finished all together, properly'.[5]

The songs and ceremonies that were performed and recorded were not, however, directly measured against Strehlow's earlier recordings, nor were contemporary performances altered in any way to match the earlier records as a way of elevating the authenticity of present practice. In the evenings, after long and tiring days full of object making, singing, and performance, the Strehlow recordings were regularly viewed and listened to. Comparisons between the past and the present were certainly there, and there was certainly an admiration for the skill and expertise of those in the past, but the current performances, which were sometimes different, were not deemed to be incorrect or inauthentic. Where the older performances revealed men using traditional artefacts, such as shields covered with red ochre and decorated with crushed plant matter that had been applied with natural adhesives, there was no hesitation to use modern techniques that had been adopted. Instead of natural ochre red, colour oxides from a local hardware store were used to decorate bodies and objects; while the plant matter used for decorations was

3 Personal Communication with Martin Hagan 28/09/2022.

4 Letters from an Arrernte and Anmatyerr men in support of funding application.

5 Personal Communication with Michael Tommy Pengart 28/09/2022.

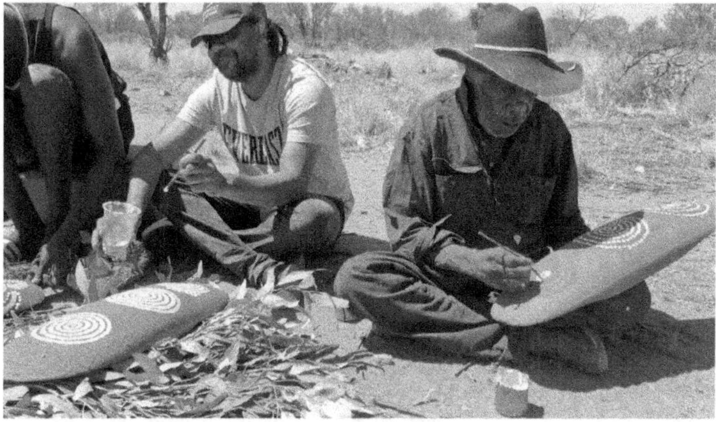

*Figure 4.1* Anmatyerr men Martin Hagan (R) and Michael Tommy (L) painting ceremonial shields for their archive at Laramba, September 2022 (photo: J. Gibson).

'traditional', this was applied with sugary water. Acrylic paints were also used to paint ceremonial shields, a medium readily adopted by Central Australian people for over five decades.

These changes in material culture were described as 'short cuts' or innovations that had emerged since the 1960s in response to life on settlements and pastoral leases, and were not thought of as detrimental to the meaning and significance of the content. Song recordings and films were also made during performances with the sounds of everyday life in the background and men danced partially clothed in modern attire. Striving for the most authentic record of the pre-contact ceremony, though, Strehlow encouraged his performers to represent their ceremonies as they would have been pre-contact and to remove from the shot any accoutrements of modernity (shoes, hats, billy cans, and so on). Songs are also recorded in places the reduced any background noise so as to capture an accurate record of the song as text, rather than a social performance.

## Full Circle

Coming full circle, the return of these audio–visual collections had unintentionally led to requests for a new salvage project. The next question, of course, was what to do with these recordings? As the project's title revealed, the Laramba community had wanted to create an archive for themselves but also for 'the nation'. The spectre of cultural endangerment that was clearly felt by many of the men, combined with years of experience with the Strehlow archive, eventually led to suggestions that the materials should be safeguarded within a museum. Martin Hagan spoke of the need to create a detailed 'archive' of these performances and complete with the type of anthropological detail that had made Strehlow's collections so useful to people today, but, rather than relying upon my abilities as a kind of community-sanctioned anthropologist to document this information, they would ensure that their voices were prominent. Regularly inserting themselves into any film and audio recordings, and standing in front of a camera or at the end of a microphone, they would recount the significance of a performance, give the names of the people regarded as owners and managers of different traditions, and list the specific places to which the traditions referred. This new collecting, while regarded as an extension or update to the Strehlow archive and other museum collections, needed to be made with an explicit collaborative model upfront. The basis of this approach would be to recognise that different and varying interests exist in this material beyond the museum, and Anmatyerr peoples have primary rights over their intangible cultural property, including the design, dances, songs, and stories.

The assembled recordings and objects, however, still lacked a home and, as the Laramba community, indeed most Central Australian Aboriginal communities, lacked the facilities to store and manage collections; other solutions were required. None of the individuals involved in the project wanted to take responsibility for the collection either as the stress of managing materials that belonged to a range of people would not only be very difficult but would contravene protocols of knowledge access and revelation. My suggestion that the shields and recordings could be kept at the Strehlow Research Centre was also repeatedly rejected, not because of any ill-feeling towards the Centre but for two explicitly stated reasons. First, it was considered best for the collection to be kept 'down south' (in the Australian capital cities) and away from politics and controversies that often coalesced around access to ceremonial knowledge in Central Australia. Even though this would mean that the collections would become geographically distant from the community, the men saw this as having its advantages. This would only be permitted, however, if the museum 'down south' agreed to their terms. There would need to be an agreement with the museum that the collection was being held in trust on behalf of the community (this provocation has yet to be tested).

Second, there was an interest in using this new collecting as a form of cultural capital to leverage new relationships with museums and the wider Australian society. Sending the collection to a major state museum was seen as a powerful way of obtaining greater acknowledgement and recognition from within the settler-colonial state and, just as importantly, brings new economic opportunities to their communities. From their perspective, Anmatyerr informants had used Strehlow's interest in recording and collecting as a way of achieving recognition and benefit during the mid-twentieth century. More recently, Anmatyerr artists innovated the use of acrylic painting to instigate the now globally recognised Aboriginal art movement (Kean 2023). As a descendent of Clifford Possum Peltharr, one of this movement's most significant painters, Hagan saw this new collecting as a continuation of his grandfather's outward-looking creativity. He recalled how this previous generation had used art exhibition openings and other cultural events in the 1980s to proudly display performances.

It is important to note that these innovations in Aboriginal art and performance in the 1980s were followed by increased interest in the repatriation of secret-sacred objects from Australian museums. The South Australian Museum, for example, had developed a *Statement on the Secret/Sacred Collection* (1986) around this time and employed anthropologists to engage with Anmatyerr and Warlpiri communities on repatriation plans. Following a trajectory like the one outlined in this chapter, the anthropologist responsible for this work, Chris Anderson, noted that, after a process of careful repatriation of many sacred objects, men from the communities of Yuendumu and Yuelamu looked for new engagements with the museum. Some of the results included the internationally successful *Dreamings: The Art of Aboriginal Australia* (1988) exhibition and, later, the South Australian Museum's eventual acquisition of the Yuendumu doors, a series of doors from the Yuendumu school that had been painted with significant local designs (Jones 2014). Around the same time members of the Yuelamu community received a Commonwealth Government grant to establish the Yuelamu Art Gallery and Museum. The museum was opened in 1988 by Hazel Hawke, the wife of then Prime Minister Bob Hawke, who praised the community for their 'decision to preserve for generations to come those traditions and skills which are unique to the culture of the Yuelamu Community'.[6] Like many small museums and keeping places, however, the operation failed after only a few years due to a lack of adequate planning and resourcing, and the collections were later distributed among families.

Returning collections is, as Anderson (1990, p. 55) wrote over three decades ago, 'first and foremost a social act', and it continues to be seen as much by Anmatyerr people today. Within this region of Central Australia alone, archival and collections' returns over several decades have led to important productive social relationships between collecting institutions and communities. This should not suggest, however, that people are not deeply aware of the problems of representation in museums. During a light-hearted exchange, as performers were being decorated at Laramba, one elder quipped, 'well, we might take Johnny to the museum now that he is painted up!' With a cheeky grin, Johnny replied, 'yes, put me behind the glass. I'll sit down behind the glass and the tourists can come visiting and they can throw me money!'[7] Years of interaction with collectors and recordists of performance have exposed the inequities of these relationships, but, at the same time, as Morphy (2022,

6 John Curtin Prime Ministerial Library, https://john.curtin.edu.au/pmportal/text/00350_5.html.

7 Personal Communication with elders at Laramba 28/09/2022.

p. 225) has commented, it has shown how 'the principles of the ethnographic museum in some ways match those – perhaps ironically – of many source communities'. Anmatyerr engagements support this view, as people work with museums to ensure that their objects are included, recognised, and valued in ways that support their cultural futures.

## Conclusion

The return of Strehlow's audio–visual recordings to Anmatyerr communities over many years has resulted in several significant responses. Anmatyerr people maintain the critical importance of their ability to speak back to the archive and expect that any recordings of their performances can be made available to present-day cultural experts and rightfully acknowledged as their cultural property. Re-integrating these recordings back into everyday life has nonetheless presented significant challenges. There are, for example, concerns about the circulation of digital objects that contain highly valued expressions of Anmatyerr cultural identity and whose distribution would traditionally be regulated between kin, in-person, and according to age, gender, and social status. Recordings of songs and ceremony that are no longer known, or no longer practiced, also now sit awkwardly within people's lives. They are reminders of colonial disruption, cultural loss, and the ever-present spectre of cultural endangerment. The return of these particular recordings has not led to a revival of these lost cultural practices, as it is often assumed that access to these archives would achieve. Instead, Anmatyerr people use these materials to look to the present, emphasise their ancestral affinities to this material, celebrate the depth of their cultural knowledge, and stress the importance of the social and cultural worlds they currently inhabit.

The lack of technological resources and infrastructure in these communities has led to long-term reliance on collecting institutions to replenish copies. Having continuing relationships with collecting institutions and their staff is not, however, necessarily considered a negative. One of the more significant responses to the return of Strehlow's audio–visual archive has been people's desire to update or add to the record. Anmatyerr people want recordings of their songs and ceremonies to be seen and understood in their context, which means understanding them as objects that have rights invested in them and must be understood in relation to the cultural context that they are embedded in within their society. Anmatyerr communities have also demonstrated an interest in using collecting institutions as a safe house or archive for posterity. Described here as 'new collecting', this is a deliberate entreaty towards a collaborative, Anmatyerr-led collecting practice made directly in response to the return of Strehlow's archive. This move has grown out of and occurred at the same time as repatriation discussions. In fact, repatriation dialogues and experiences have opened spaces for these kinds of good-faith collaborations.

## References

Anderson, C. 1990, 'Repatriation of Cultural Property: A Social Process', *Museum International*, vol. 42, no. 1, pp. 54–55.

Board of the South Australian Museum. 1986, *South Australian Museum Statement on the Secret/Sacred Collection*, South Australian Museum, Adelaide, accessed from www.samuseum.sa.gov.au/Upload/files-about/secret-sacred_collection-policy.pdf.

Bolton, L. 2015, 'An Ethnography of Repatriation: Engagements with Erromango, Vanuatu', in *The International Handbooks of Museum Studies*, John Wiley and Sons, Ltd, pp. 229–248, accessed November 18, 2022, from https://onlinelibrary.wiley.com/doi/abs/10.1002/9781118829059.wbihms410.

Bracknell, C. 2019, 'Connecting Indigenous Song Archives to Kin, Country and Language', *Journal of Colonialism and Colonial History*, vol. 20, no. 2.

Bray, T.L. 1996, 'Repatriation, Power Relations and the Politics of the Past', *Antiquity*, vol. 70, no. 268, pp. 440–444.

Campbell, G. 2014, 'Song as Artefact: The Reclaiming of Song Recordings Empowering Indigenous Stakeholders – and the Recordings Themselves', in A. Harris (ed), *Circulating Cultures: Exchanges of Australian Indigenous Music, Dance and Media*, The Australian National University, Canberra, pp. 101–128.

Clifford, J. 1997, 'Museums as Contact Zones', in *Routes: Travel and Translation in the Late Twentieth Century*, Harvard University Press, Cambridge, pp. 188–219.

Conway, R.J. 2021, *Djalkiri: Yolŋu Art, Collaborations and Collections*, Sydney University Press, University of Sydney, NSW, accessed from https://ezproxy.deakin.edu.au/login?url=https://search.ebscohost.com/login.aspx?direct=trueanddb=nlebkandAN=2918805andsite=eds-liveandscope=site.

Duwell, M. & Dixon, R.M.W. 1994, *Little Eva at Moonlight Creek, and other Aboriginal Song Poems*, University of Queensland Press, St. Lucia, Queensland.

Gibson, J. 2020, *Ceremony Men: Making Ethnography and the Return of the Strehlow Collection*, State University of New York Press, Albany.

Glowczewski, B. 2020, *Indigenising Anthropology with Guattari and Deleuze*, Edinburgh University Press, Edinburgh.

Gunderson, F., Lancefield, R.C. & Woods, B. (eds). 2018, *The Oxford Handbook of Musical Repatriation*, Oxford University Press, Oxford, accessed October 16, 2018, from www.oxfordhandbooks.com/view/10.1093/oxfordhb/9780190659806.001.0001/oxfordhb-9780190659806.

Hersey, S. & Cohen, H. 2004, 'Visulaising Anthropology: Ethnography Documentary and the Films of T.G.H. Strehlow', in *Traditions in the Midst of Change: Proceedings of the Strehlow Conference 2002*, Strehlow Research Centre, Alice Springs, pp. 177–183.

Hilder, T.R. 2012, 'Repatriation, Revival and Transmission: The Politics of a Sámi Musical Heritage', *Ethnomusicology Forum*, vol. 21, no. 2, pp. 161–179.

Hill, B. 2003, *Broken Song: T.G.H. Strehlow and Aboriginal Possession*, Random House, Milsons Point, NSW.

Jackson, J.B. 2007, 'The Paradoxical Power of Endangerment Traditional Native American Dance and Music in Eastern Oklahoma', *World Literature Today*, vol. 81, no. 5, pp. 37–41.

Jonaitis, A. & Glass, A. 2010, *The Totem Pole: An Intercultural History*, University of Washington Press, Seattle, accessed January 20, 2020, from https://trove.nla.gov.au/version/47211620.

Jones, P.G. 2014, *Behind the Doors: An Art History from Yuendumu*, South Australian Museum in association with Wakefield Press, Adelaide, SA.

Jorgensen, D. 2010, 'Simulating the Sacred in Theodore Strehlow's Songs of Central Australia', *The Bible and Critical Theory*, vol. 6, no. 2, pp. 22.2–22.10.

Kean, J. 2023, *Dot Circle and Frame: The Making of Papunya Tula art*. Upswell, Perth.

Kenny, A. 2013, *The Aranda's Pepa: An Introduction to Carl Strehlow's Masterpiece Die Aranda- und Loritja-Stämme in Zentral-Australien (1907–1920)*, ANU E Press, Canberra.

Kowal, E. 2015, *Trapped in the Gap: Doing Good in Indigenous Australia*, Berghahn Books, New York.

Marett, A. 2010, 'Vanishing Songs: How Musical Extinctions Threaten the Planet', *Ethnomusicology Forum* 19, no. 2 (November 2010). pp. 249–262, https://doi.org/10.1080/17411912.2010.508238.

Michaels, E. 1985, 'Constraints on Knowledge in an Economy of Oral Information', *Current Anthropology*, vol. 26, no. 4, pp. 505–510.

Morphy, H. & Gibson, J.M. 2022, 'Special Section: Leading Thinkers in the Field – Howard Morphy', *Museum Worlds*, vol. 10, no. 1, pp. 218–229.

Peers, L. & Brown, A. 2003, 'Collaboration in Exhibitions: Toward a Dialogic Paradigm', in L. Peers & A. Brown (eds), *Museums and Source Communities: A Routledge Reader*, Routledge, New York, pp. 153–170.

Perkins, R. 2016, 'Songs to Live By: The Arrernte Women's Project is Preserving Vital Songs and Culture', *The Monthly*, no. July, pp. 1–3.

Phillips, R. 2003, 'Community Collaboration in Exhibitions: Introduction', in L. Peers & A. Brown (eds), *Museums and Source Communities: A Routledge Reader*, Routledge, London, pp. 155–170.

Pink, O. 1936, 'The Landowners of the Northern Division of the Aranda tribe, Central Australia', *Oceania*, vol. 6, no. 3, pp. 275–305.

Smith, L. 2022, 'Historical Fish Collection Catapults Aboriginal Fishing Methods onto International Stage', *ABC News*, accessed December 2, 2022, from www.abc.net.au/news/2022-11-30/menang-noongar-historic-fish-colletion-london-scotland-museums/101713456.

Smith, R. 2009, '"Stuff at the Core of Land Rights Claims": The Strehlow Collection', *Journal of Northern Territory History*, no. 20, pp. 75–93.

Strehlow, T.G.H. 1947, *Aranda Traditions*, 2nd ed., Johnson Reprint, New York.

Strehlow, T.G.H. 1965, *Book XXXVI: Field Diary (36) 1965*, Strehlow Research Centre, Alice Springs.

Strehlow, T.G.H. 1971, *Songs of Central Australia*, Angus and Robertson, Sydney.

Sutton, P. 1988, *Dreamings: The Art of Aboriginal Australia*, 2nd ed., Viking, Ringwood.

Treloyn, S., Martin, M. & Charles, R. 2016, 'Cultural Precedents for the Repatriation of Legacy Song Records to Communities of Origin', *Australian Aboriginal Studies*, vol. 2016–January, no. 2, pp. 94–103.

Turpin, M. 2014, 'Song-poetry of Central Australia: Sustaining Traditions', in N. Burenhult, A. Holmer, A. Karlsson, H. Lundström, & J. Svantesson (eds), *Language Documentation and Description, Special Issue on Humanities of the Lesser-known: New Directions in the Description, Documentation and Typology of Endangered Languages and Musics*, SOAS, London, pp. 15–36.

Wanambi, W., Skerritt, H. & McDonald, K. 2022, *Madayin: Eight Decades of Aboriginal Australian Art from Yirrkala, Kluge-Ruhe Aboriginal Art Collection*, University of Virginia, Vriginia.

# 5 Transformative Collaborations in Australian Ethnographic Collections

In the currently established literature about decolonisation as a political and social objective within the museum sector, the repatriation of cultural heritage is a central concern. Museums, and indeed all collecting institutions, are under increasing pressure to find ways of decolonising their practice, and the repatriation of cultural objects and human remains, along with the protection of archaeological and historical sites, has become emblematic of the decolonial process. These objectives are often presented as solutions to present inequities and much needed responses to histories of colonial violence and appropriation. In this final substantive chapter, I consider these calls to decolonise and, while noting the significance of these movements, address the limitations of the approach. As has been demonstrated in previous chapters, many Aboriginal communities in Australia now confidently assert their rights to their cultural heritage collections but also draw upon and utilise collecting institutions in dynamic ways. Rather than making an argument for the complete extraction of their collections from collecting institutions, they argue for their own controlled systems of knowledge, access, and revelation. This opens the possibility of managing the value of collections in a changing future. As this book has demonstrated, these collections often contain truly entangled objects that play a continuing role in the value-creation processes. Changing museum and government policies have facilitated the return of some objects to Central Australia, and in some cases, local storehouses, such as the Strehlow Research Centre, have created important 'middle spaces' where the necessarily slow, local Indigenous assessment of the material and its reincorporation into the community can be considered.

Wholesale repatriation of cultural artefacts is clearly not always a priority and nor is it often practical or desirable. As important as the rhetoric of repatriation has been, it can paralyse and close off thinking about new and diverse ways forward in terms of valuing, using, and caring for cultural collections. What links practices of repatriation to theories of decolonisation is the implicit notion (or expectation) that the return of cultural materials might reverse, or at least ameliorate, processes of colonial history. The entanglement of collections, meaning their diverse histories and the different experiences of

DOI: 10.4324/9781003158752-5

diverse source communities in dealing with collectors and collecting institutions, is, however, generally deemphasised in this discourse. At worst, source communities are imagined as living in an imagined past, and object restitution will automatically aid the continuation of unchanged cultural practices. There is little room for imagining a future in which museums and communities work together to support Indigenous aspirations. At its best though, a spirit of cooperation emerges after decades of Indigenous activism, advocacy, and policy change in Australia reflecting contemporary needs and aspirations. This need not exclude the possibility, however, that, in some cases, repatriation will be the best and ethically most appropriate outcome but rather points to the problem of simply equating repatriation with decolonisation.

As repeatedly stated throughout this book, repatriation has been an incredibly important driver in the Indigenous cultural heritage domain. The Australian Government has supported the repatriation of Australian Indigenous ancestral remains from overseas for over 30 years across nine countries. More than 1,600 ancestors have been returned to Australia (Office for the Arts n.d.). Nonetheless, parallel postrepatriation activities need to be imagined alongside ongoing repatriation dialogues.

Re-imagining the anthropological, ethnographic, or 'world culture museums' is now a considerable preoccupation in this field, but it has a long history. In the late twentieth century, anthropology as a discipline went through a well-documented period of representational crisis (Hymes 1972; Clifford & Marcus 1986). In settler colonies, such as Australia, the United States, New Zealand, and Canada, where anthropologists and the objects of their study stand in such close spatial proximity, tensions and inequities quickly came sharply into focus. Out of the political progressivism of the late 1960s emerged deeper postcolonial critiques, and more and more Indigenous peoples increasingly began to read the earlier ethnographies that had been written about them and make enquiries about related collections. In Australia and New Zealand, changes to the way ethnographic museums were managed came further to the fore in the 1980s when 'Indigenous Australians and Melanesians, among others, entered museums and brought with them a series of ideas about the meaning of objects that . . . unsettled and irretrievably altered the ways in which ethnographic collections can be imagined and understood' (Bolton 2001, p. 218). These increasing Indigenous engagements with collections over a number of decades has, in the words of Yuwaalaraay scholar Jilda Andrews, offered all involved 'extraordinary and important' opportunities (2022, p. 225). These have also urged collecting institutions to potentially become far more socially responsible cultural agents underpinned by, and responsive to, the values of the people they once objectified. But is the argument for decolonisation an extension of these experiences or something else altogether?

Decolonisation is now applied to all sorts of political acts and used as shorthand for any move that might acknowledge or support the actions of those negatively affected by colonialism. As one social media meme joked, decolonising is 'the hot sauce you can put on everything'.[1] The concept is now so overused that it is difficult to gauge its usefulness. Moreover, the term has its origins in academic and professional discourse; although it is used by Indigenous activists, it is not often evidenced in the everyday speech of Indigenous stakeholder communities from Central Australia discussed in this book. Alternatively, people will speak of having their 'Law' respected and recognised, their voices heard, and their rights of cultural heritage upheld. They want the agency and pride of their ancestors to be acknowledged and recognition that, as the descendants of these people and the land they originate from, they deserve a say in creating new value from these collections. The relationship between museums and communities in these contexts is, therefore, framed in a way that rarely resorts to binary colonial/decolonial periodisation or the politics embedded in the term decolonisation. Instead, it evokes themes of endurance, kinship, and alternate knowledge systems.

In this chapter, I argue for the value of the museum as a dialogical space to develop new practices for ethical engagements with coloniality. Drawing upon my own experiences as a traveller between community, academic, and museum worlds – an individual whose focus has most often been the ethnographic collections – I write this chapter as an ethnographer keenly interested in the circulation of cultural heritage as it moves across and within different regimes of value. The responsibility of the ethnographer, as I see it, is to document the way these relationships play out in practice. When thinking through these issues, I have adopted a relational ethnographic methodology by taking the *field* of repatriation and return as my objects of study. The focal point in this chapter, then, is not necessarily a particular Indigenous group, or a particular institution, but the field of interactions that exist between museums, Aboriginal people, collectors, and researchers (including myself). This approach is used to accentuate the relational and processual nature of social reality and avoid recourse to roughly hewn categories that conceive of the social world as made up of collections of isolated groups. To use a collections metaphor, this approach avoids visualising the world as 'a vast collection of isolated entities stacked side-by-side like so many jarred specimens on laboratory shelves' (Desmond 2014, p. 551) and instead looks for the intertwining interconnections between individual actors, people, and institutions. Groups are intertwined with one another, and the point of fieldwork is to show how things hang together in a web of mutual influence or support. This *field* of museum and community interactions has been theorised and described in other contexts as a 'contact zone' (Clifford 1997; Krmpotich & Peers 2013) and comprises different people and groups in relation, occupying qualitatively different positions.

## Indigeneity in Contemporary Museum Management

In Australia, the current surge of interest in Aboriginal peoples' cultural knowledge, ontologies, and practices has been mystifying to some scholars, particularly anthropologists who have been engaging with Aboriginal and Torres Strait Islander communities for decades. The Conference for Museum Anthropologists (COMA), for example, operated between 1979 and 1990 and emerged partly in response to the 1978 UNESCO Regional Seminar on the Role of Museums in Preserving Indigenous Cultures, held in Adelaide, marking a 'turning point in the relationship between Indigenous communities and the museum sector in Australia, as well as in Oceania between Pacific Island nations and the museums of Australia and New Zealand' (Stanton 2011). Many of the issues raised at COMA meetings inspired discussions at comparable conferences overseas where museum-based anthropologists were actively promoting the central role of Indigenous communities in the custodianship and representation of institutional collections. Combined with the significant role played by Indigenous curators, these engagements led to dramatic changes in museological practice and a related revitalisation of state and national museums across the continent through new exhibitions, fresh engagements, and additional appointments. There has also been increased Indigenous representation throughout the museum world – in collections, at the senior management level, and on boards of trustees. Aboriginal scholar and activist, Gary Foley (2002, p. 11), noted that, by the early 2000s, Indigenous Australians were, therefore, 'much more assertive in their dealings with the museum and in their quest to alter the meaning and purpose of the institution'.

In Southern and Eastern Australia, where most state museum collections reside, years of violence and murder at the hands of settlers in the eighteenth and nineteenth centuries were followed by enforced missionisation, wardship, and assimilation that attacked the social reproduction of local cultures. Unlike in Central and Northern Australia where Indigenous peoples make up over 30% of the population, Aboriginal peoples in the south are a minority among ethnic minorities. Nonetheless, across Australia forms of state recognition are typically targeted at those able to persuasively articulate a clear thread of continuous 'traditional' laws and cultural practices to precolonial customs and ancestors. Even where there is no legal imperative to do this, interactions between Aboriginal peoples and others are often conditioned by it (Neale in press). This field, where Indigenous and non-Indigenous people participate in ascribing value and meaning to cultural heritage collections is, therefore, at the heart of understanding contemporary settler-colonial articulations. As Neale (in press) argues, the sanctioning of these processes of recognition produces both *affordances* and *foreclosures* for different individuals and groups. The primary terms around which Aboriginal cultural heritage is figured – 'tradition' and 'culture' – are, however, fraught and contested. Early anthropological investments in these terms as the core of social reality ensured that they became the battleground for subsequent debates regarding not only the distinctiveness of social groups but also the persistence of identity through contact with others. The dominance of 'tradition' as a framework for recognising Aboriginality and Indigeneity more generally intensified through the post-1970s era of liberal multiculturalism and its aftermath. Progressive reforms carried assumptions that defined who and what was eligible as Indigenous (Merlan 2006). Ideologies of indigenousness persist today in many settler-colonial nations, forcing Indigenous peoples to respond to external images of themselves to gain financial or political leverage. Those who do not fit such images are less likely to be afforded these opportunities. Anthropologists have, thus, become more reflexive about this ideology and, rather than policing the semantic terrain of 'Indigenous tradition', prefer to better understand the contingent and changing practice of its 'articulation' (Clifford 2001).

Museums, and other institutions of cultural heritage, are now critical institutional and interpersonal contact zones where these articulations are made. These enmeshments and encounters are now common as museums are expected to consult, work with, employ, and subcontract specific Indigenous peoples and groups; repatriation initiatives are key sites of exchange. In these contexts, the staff of collecting institutions – a group that is disproportionately non-Indigenous – engages with Aboriginal peoples regarding policies, prescriptions, moralities, and interests. The diverse aims of Aboriginal employment, Aboriginal institutional autonomy, individual self-determination, reconciliation policies, cultural revitalisation, social justice, risk mitigation, and cultural restoration can all be at work in each context, and the relative importance of each can be a matter of accord or disagreement. The high stakes of these performances are, at least in part, set by non-Indigenous peoples who seek out an Aboriginal organisation or person to provide legitimacy. Here, as elsewhere, Indigenous peoples face the difficult request to help amend the ills of settler-colonialism. In such moments, it is important to critique these articulations, affordances, and foreclosures to understand how their costs and benefits are differentially distributed and what they make possible. On the one hand, these arrangements ask for Indigenous peoples to actively and creatively negotiate the anachronistic expectations of others to succeed, and on the other hand, for those able to meet these expectations, such situations offer new opportunities with both state and non-state interests. In Australia, Indigenous peoples' rights to cultural heritage are increasingly recognised within settler institutions, albeit in limited ways. In the cultural heritage sector, Aboriginal peoples are increasingly acknowledged as stakeholders or partners in decision-making, and there is a recognition that Indigenous knowledge resides in archives and collections. Subsequently, Indigenous rights of access and, to some degree, control over these materials are conceived as being important, if not a moral responsibility of a postcolonial institution.

The Australian Institute of Aboriginal and Torres Strait Islander Studies (AIATSIS) 'Return of Cultural Heritage' programme, an initiative that has successfully negotiated the repatriation of hundreds of cultural objects from international museums back to Australia (Johnston et al. 2021), is now beginning to explore Indigenous-led frameworks for collections governance and stewardship. As a leading institution responsible for Australian Indigenous cultural heritage research and archiving, AIATSIS recognise the need to elevate Indigenous governance. In short, the institutionalisation of a particular currency – in this case, values and mechanisms for the inheritance and custodianship of cultural materials – produces many possibilities, including the transformation of postcolonial institutions. What is important about these moves is that it goes beyond the reclamation of objects to the realisation that Indigenous knowledge is not simply tied to novel or esoteric readings of objects but has governance-value. Collaborative models of collections research and exhibition development have been a key feature of what Phillips (2005, p. 87) has referred to as the 'second museum age' for decades now, but, perhaps, the next 'age' will involve a further transformation of the institution itself. The notion of transformation is presently an emergent theme within global museum studies literature (Coombes & Phillips 2020; Brus & Zillinger 2021; Gibson 2019; Wergin 2021).

A key argument of this chapter is that museums now need to accept this governance-value and move beyond both the simplistic rhetoric of repatriation and the platitudes of decolonisation. Critiques of settler-colonialism and its effects on cultural, epistemological, and territorial relationships are now well-established and provide the backdrop for current discussions about the task of decolonisation. What is now required, as philosopher Simone Bignall argues, are new relationship practices and better opportunities to reconstruct alternative modes of social existence through a 'collaborative politics of material transformation' (Bignall 2010, pp. 3–4). This language of *transformation* and *collaboration*, which the ethnographic contents of this book also attest to, is now being expressed in the strategy documents of some of Australia's major museums. The Melbourne Museum, for example, articulates the need to move 'beyond tokenism' in the form of Indigenous employment and inclusion (a point echoed by Wayne Modest) and the need to 'deeply transform' the institution through the embedding of 'the values of First Peoples communities into the fabric of our organisation' (CRANAplus 2021, p. 11). The following is an attempt to unpack what some of these transformations might look like.

## How Museums Are Understood

Museums are of course understood in a variety of different ways across the Indigenous communities of Australia. In Central Australia, the notion of 'the museum', therefore, has its own specific connotations that stem from the diverse relationships that have existed between individuals, communities, and collecting practices (predominantly anthropological and art focused) over the past 150 years. There has been very little ethnographic work conducted on this question; however, several examples from the literature and my own experience might help us come to a better understanding. One of the first researchers to really engage with issues pertaining to the collection of Central Australian Aboriginal objects of cultural significance was Fred Myers. Having witnessed the rise of global interest in Western Desert acrylic painting in the late 1970s, Myers engaged in detailed conversations with Pintupi men about the collection and display of their art and objects in Western collecting institutions. While consulting with these men on the suitability of exhibiting and storing their sacred designs and objects, Myers noted how 'museums' were considered a more appropriate place than art galleries. Ronnie Tjampitjinpa, for example, initially agreed that paintings with sacred designs could be displayed in a 'museum' but changed this decision when it was explained that the artworks could be accessed by a wider public, including women and children from his community.

> I think that Tjampitjinpa's initial confusion had to do with my use of the word 'museum', as I asked him if these paintings could be shown in one. The word museum to him is *nuseum*, a word the Pintupi at least identify with the men's sacred storehouse – where the similarity would seem to make it an acceptable place to show!
>
> (Myers 2017, p. 11)

Similar sentiments were evident in my discussions with Warlpiri man Amos Eagan at Lajamanu in 2008. I had been in and out of his communities (Papunya, Lajamanu, and Yuendumu) for several years, working on projects to provide better access to local cultural heritage collections kept in museums, libraries, and archives. When discussing notions of 'archiving' and finding appropriate places for the storage of cultural knowledge, Amos (like many of the Central Australian men I discussed this with) would find parallels from his own cultural context. He described the sacred places in his country where both cultural knowledge and objects resided, as akin to the Western notion of a 'museum'. These were physical places that, like museums and featured levels of security, were surrounded by protective forms of the convention such as limited revelation, seclusion, and rules around access. The contents were not only valued for aesthetic reasons, as in an art gallery, but were objects of further considerable cultural gravitas, local historical significance, and ancestral importance. Other elders have also often noted the vital importance of holding cultural knowledge and objects for it to be 'passed on' across the generations. From within this Aboriginal framework, museums might only be successful (or legitimate) if they hold cultural knowledge and possessions in trust for future use. My discussions with Anmatyerr people about the collections made of their performative traditions by the anthropologist Theodor George Heinrich (T. G. H.) Strehlow similarly revealed this emphasis on ensuring ongoing access and governance (Gibson 2020). The notion of storing and caring for cultural knowledge and objects clearly had parallels with museums, despite radically different notions of ownership.

How contemporary Central Australian Aboriginal people value and treat objects of cultural significance was made clear to me during a visit to the home of Rodney Cook in 2019. Cook lived with his family in a town camp on the outskirts of Alice Springs; while I had discussed what museums held that might be of interest to him and his family for several years, on this occasion, I was invited to see his personal collections. I sat at the rear of the home on the ground, while the family dog sniffed at my sandals, and the women and children were told to move to the other side of the building. Soon after Rodney appeared with a collection of 'things' wrapped in a blanket, at other people's homes, I had been shown small photographic collections – often copies of the late nineteenth century and early twentieth century photos taken by various anthropologists – but, on this occasion, the collection being shared was of material culture. The items were carefully packed and cared for; a difficult task given the poor housing conditions, extreme climate, and mobility of people in Central Australian Aboriginal communities. Contained in the blanket were numerous objects and adornments that once belonged to his father and grandfather, many made of hair string, feather, stone, and wood. Other items included ochred animal bones wrapped in European cloth and human hair string, all prudently parcelled in the best materials available – plastic shopping bags – and stored in a calico carrier (Fieldnotes, 23 February 2019). As we sat cross-legged, peering into bags, and discussing each remarkable item that Cook had kept safe for decades, we shared a deep comradeship and concern for Anmatyerr cultural heritage. Contrary to the derogatory yet common opinion that Aboriginal people were careless with material possessions, the care with which Cook packaged and stored his materials was evident. The objects had been secreted away due to their high cultural value; while it was a privilege to see them, there was a clear lesson to be learned for the cultural heritage sector.

I had only ever previously encountered objects like these in the austere, climate-controlled stores of museums or within the faded pages of older anthropological texts. To see them handled in this way, residing with people, in their homes, and valued as personal and familial treasures, I removed them from the realm of anthropological curiosity. Cook's generosity helped me understand that practices of care persisted in ways that were generally missed, indeed hidden, from mainstream attention. People did not generally share these insights. Museum practitioners who visited Central Australian communities (who were mostly concerned with collections held elsewhere) rarely asked questions about local collection practices. This experience with Cook, and other similar interactions since, urged me to rethink the way conventional museums and collecting institutions operated. I wondered how museum policies, practices, ethics, and behaviours could be challenged or changed by Indigenous source communities rather than simply deaccessioning objects and then disengaging from communities. What were the prospects for shifting museums in line with Indigenous aspirations? What if we sought out a way to radically change larger social structures and practices in accordance with Indigenous ontologies and epistemologies?

These questions were not borne of a desire to entirely negate the activist push to decolonise, even dismantle, museums but to honour the message of relationality, which is often expressed by diverse Indigenous stakeholders. As one Gunditj community member from Southwestern Victoria, explain it: 'I see the Museum as the heart, and the communities are the bloodline to the heart, keeping it going' (CRANAplus 2021, p. 24). Representatives of the La Perouse Local Aboriginal Land Council in Sydney have also publicly spoken about their desire not to dismantle museums and see all their cultural heritages repatriated but to positively engage with collecting institutions. As Ray Ingrey has reflected in his community's negotiations with the Cambridge Museum of Archaeology and Anthropology over four spears collected by James Cook in 1770, elders decided not to pursue repatriation but greater access and collaboration.

> When Elders in the 90s started to campaign for the return of significant cultural objects . . . they came to the conclusion that it would be very difficult to change the laws [regarding repatriation] . . . they realized that if they [the spears] weren't held in a museum-grade facility, we wouldn't be able to look at them today.
>
> (Ingrey quoted in Butler 2022)

The current impetus then is to foster positive relationships with both domestic and international institutions to preserve and provide access to objects via loan agreements and ensure that younger generations can 'showcase' their continued connections.

> Dharawal Elders have a long-term aspiration to be able to showcase not only the spears but other important artefacts to our people and showcase our ongoing culture and connection to places like Kamay here.
>
> (Ingrey quoted in Butler 2022)

In early 2022, the four spears were loaned to the Chak Chau Wing Museum at the University of Sydney for the purposes of community access and a public exhibition over three months. For now, the community has expressed that they will be 'happy' to send the spears back to Cambridge at the conclusion of the loan but are eager to continue 'conversations' about greater access via on longer-term loans (Butler 2022).

The expectation among many communities now is that museums will be more responsive to changing social and cultural needs. As generally conservative and cautious institutions, museums require the provocations of activists, community members, and art practitioners, but they can also learn from their often long-term and meaningful engagements with diverse Indigenous stakeholder groups.

## Decolonisation and Transformative Collaborations

The cultural heritage and collections sector has been a critical arena in which debates about decolonisation and indigenisation have played out in the public sphere. At the heart of these discussions is an acknowledgement of the need to challenge the interests and paradigms of the dominant cultural group, particularly white colonisers. These ideas have their roots in the movements across colonised states to expunge the colonial experience and restore authority and dignity to local and Indigenous populations. At the cultural level too, the related discourse of postcolonialism has contributed to strong arguments about the need to ensure that systems of communication, expression, and performance are the people's own and not the culturally 'alienating' and 'imposed' ones of the colonial order (Betts 2012, p. 30). This may involve numerous strategies, including the restoration and celebration of marginalised languages, the reinstatement of Indigenous place names, land reclamation, the return of cultural collections, and the elevation of Indigenous systems of governance (and many other strategies) to wrestle back power.

This decolonial turn has its roots in the multidisciplinary body of scholarship that examined the impacts and legacies of colonialism, which gained momentum in the 1990s, often under the banner of postcolonialism. This work raised questions about the potential liberation of subaltern and colonised peoples 'from the knowledge system of the post-Enlightenment West' (Betts 2012, p. 34) and questioned whether museums, as institutions of coloniality, could commence more positive cultural shifts towards inclusion and recognition, a movement now generally thought of as 'new museology' (Krouse 2006). The general impetus of the postcolonial move was to pluralise the history of global political modernity. Postcolonial theorist Dipesh Chakrabarty, for example, wrote that European systems of thought need not be discarded entirely but that 'this thought – which is now everybody's heritage and affects us all' could be 'renewed from and for the margins' (2000, p. 16). The growth of research into Indigenous methodologies, founded upon the notion that knowledge exists within a set of relationships and responsibilities rooted in place or land, has concurrently had significant impacts on the field (Phillips 2011; Chalmers 2017). Taken together, theories of postcoloniality and decolonisation, along with Indigenous methodologies, have had a significant impact on the wider cultural heritage sector in Australia and beyond by de-centring Eurocentric approaches and re-centring marginalised ones.

Given all the complexities associated with repatriating Indigenous cultural materials, James Clifford is right to point out that the process of 'decolonising' collections will not be an 'all or nothing, once and for all, transition' (2013, p. 302). As I hope that this book has evidenced, the entangled and often intertwined histories of these collections can make their reintegration and revivification in contemporary social lives inherently complex. There are of course uncomfortable histories and imbalances of power and status between collectors, makers, institutions, and communities, but collecting institutions are precisely among the main sources of evidence (along with oral histories) for helping us uncover and scrutinise these difficult colonial pasts. Collections help us better understand the histories of violence and coercion but also of cooperation, resistance, and negotiation, making for a much more complex and precise understanding of history. As colonialism severed – or at least attempted to sever – Indigenous relationships between people, places, stories, and objects; then, a decolonial approach to museums (and cultural heritage more generally) ought to have as one of its major objectives of the reconnecting and re-braiding of relationships. Building upon the achievements of Indigenous methodologies too, it ought to see researchers and institutions move towards greater professional and ethical accountability.

The revitalising impulse of these ideas is unmistakable, but decolonisation may not be the best term to encapsulate this momentum. Seminal scholar of settler-colonial studies Patrick Wolfe described settler-colonialism as an enduring 'structure' and not an 'event', thus highlighting deeply rooted inter-relationships that cannot be easily disentangled. A movement from settler-colonialism to a post-colonial or decolonial era, therefore, will require significant structural change, but even then, the multiple dimensions and non-singular forms of knowledge contained in the systems, practices, and contents of museums make unravelling these structures problematic. As a museum anthropologist, this is the approach that I take. Settler-colonialism, including acts of collecting, has damaged relationships and fragmented the world, and as such, it will now require a collective effort to reassemble the pieces. However, this will not result in definitive, resurrected, or pure form. Again, as James Clifford has written, decolonising collections will not be an 'all or nothing, once and for all, transition' (2013, p. 302) but a process of ongoing dialogue, interaction, inventiveness, and a reconstituting of relationships between people, objects, and place.

Perhaps, then, we need to think of the prospect of decolonisation of cultural heritage as a provocation rather than a resolution. It is for similar reasons that philosopher Simone Bignall has introduced the term excolonialism (exit colonialism) to designate an ideally decolonised future community that is perpetually 'yet to come'. She acknowledges that 'postcolonial' nations and institutions remain invested predominantly in settler interests and, thus, argues for a conceptual shift away from theories of social transformation that emphasises conflict to positive forces of 'engagement' and 'transforming communities' (2014, p. 343). Without ignoring the realities of conflict or the significance of dissent in political life, she emphasises collaboration as a constructive and transformative social force. Conflictual models, she goes on to argue, can lead to a somewhat alienating experience of fighting 'someone else's fight' as a 'supporter', and so can diminish the general 'communal responsibility' required to make a lasting social change (2014, p. 347). As much as museums are instruments of any given society, they are also complex entities defined by shared histories and contemporary coexistence.

Some of the collaborative transformations needed to better care for and manage Indigenous cultural heritage and collections are already underway. As an example, just in the final months of 2021, a small collection of culturally significant objects (17 in total) were returned to Arrernte, Warlpiri, and Warumungu peoples by the University of Virginia's Kluge-Ruhe collection, and the remains of numerous Kaurna ancestors were returned by the South Australian Museum to a new, purpose-built re-burial site on the fringes of Adelaide. Initiatives like this are becoming a permanent feature of museum practice in settler-colonial contexts. Fitting with the theme of this book, though, it is important to ask what more can and ought to be done beyond acts of repatriation. How can collecting institutions, their practices, and relationships be further transformed? Given the entangled relations with the colonial past – of extraction, appropriation, negotiation, and (mis)representation – collecting institutions are powerful sites for re-working or working through these histories and fashioning better futures. As Wayne Modest (2019, p. 13) has argued, 'it may precisely be with the master's tools that we can do the work of dismantling the master's house'.

## Diverse Values, Frameworks, and Expectations

The first observation is simple: acknowledge the diversity of Indigenous epistemologies, values, and ontologies. Collecting institutions have historically privileged Western epistemologies, value systems, and either marginalised or simplified Indigenous ones. In recent decades, however, libraries, archives, and museums have all produced various guidelines and protocols for managing Indigenous cultural heritage. These guidelines, while covering practical issues of access, control, preservation, and management of collections, each also aim to mediate relationships between Indigenous and non-Indigenous peoples. These protocols, although premised on a rights agenda and meant as a way of recognising Indigenous structures of authority and governance, have their limitations. Principally, they cannot adequately represent or respond to the enormous diversity of Indigenous Australian societies. As Morphy (2015) has argued, there is a danger of building a dualistic opposition between Indigenous and non-Indigenous Australians, thus encouraging the idea that one set of protocols will apply equally to all Indigenous Australians. While, in many cases, the writers of protocols have been scrupulous in trying to avoid the creation of a pan-Aboriginal identity, the very nature of the areas that they cover can be taken as a general inventory of differences. Developing localised and ethnographically informed understandings of the often highly specific relationships that different Indigenous communities have to different objects held in collections is, therefore, paramount.

If there is one thing that Indigenous people have taught settler-colonists who have been willing to listen, it is that all of us (indeed every 'thing') exist within relational networks. Colonialism is a force that has often done damage to or severed these relationships, and the work of mending or rebraiding the threads has become a contemporary preoccupation. The recognition of Indigenous knowledge helps us see that these networks continue to exist or have the potential to regrow and, thus, need to be foregrounded in future policy and practice. There is now important work to be done to challenge the privileging of Western epistemologies and value systems, and permit once marginalised Indigenous values and ontologies to shape the institution. Indigenous scholars, and many of those who have worked with Indigenous peoples, have used these insights to develop and advocate for ways of working that honours this relationality. Museums, such as Te Papa in New Zealand, have led the way in terms of radical reforms, embracing a bicultural approach to all aspects of the museum's operations. Rather than prioritising the dominant Western perspective when describing, cataloguing, and displaying objects in the museum and its online platforms, everything is co-developed and co-managed with the source (Māori) culture. However, as Conal McCarthy comments:

> there seem to be limits to what can be achieved within the structure of metropolitan and national institutions . . . To a large degree, orthodox museum practices have been challenged, modified and adapted, but new practices based on Indigenous paradigms and epistemologies have only recently begun to emerge.
>
> (McCarthy 2011, p. 245)

As with my examples from the Strehlow Research Centre in earlier chapters, McCarthy goes on to note that 'the most far-reaching changes to museum practice have occurred in small regional museums enmeshed in reciprocal relationships with local communities' (2011, p. 245). The Strehlow Research Centre has, for example, trialled the partial reorganisation of the collections store so that objects, once arranged by object type or size, are now regrouped according to underlying cultural associations based on their relationships to ancestors, clan estates, and/or ceremonial events. This change in classification, nomenclature, and spatial reorganising is, however, only possible when there is deep collaborative work undertaken with a specific source community. In this case, members of the Arrernte community were curators and collection managers working in the centre, making decisions following years of detailed conversations with elders. The objects related to the sites were either boxed together or kept near each other so that cultural linkages could be maintained, documented, and noted with links to past and present individuals with rights to these assemblages. In essence, there was an attempt to honour the relational ontology of Arrernte peoples.

For Central Australian Aboriginal people, the management of collections needs to be handled in a way that is consistent with their understanding of cultural knowledge and materials. As I have outlined elsewhere, this is often done by insisting that the dual roles of a cultural 'manager' and 'owner' are acknowledged (Gibson 2019). Described as a 'ritual-based system of formalised complementary filiation', this means that the 'managers' of this cultural knowledge and material (referred to as *kwertengerle* in Arrernte) will work in concert with the 'traditional owners' (*apmerek-artweye*), meaning those that have inherited ownership along patrilineal lines. The managers play an important role in helping owners maintain the integrity and long-term transmission and circulation of their objects, rituals, songs, dances, and so on. Likened to a 'governance structure' by some Warlpiri people (Pawu-Kurlpurlurnu, Holmes & Box 2008), these complementary tasks ensure that everyone within this network of relatedness has a role to play. When assimilated into these local frameworks of social relatedness, museums and their staff are increasingly being regarded by Central Australian people as 'working for' them in a manner, not unlike a *kwertengerle*. This is like what Myers (1986) observed among other groups in Central Australia, who regarded Western forms of authority as now being responsible for 'looking after' or 'caring for' Aboriginal people and their interests. Many Aboriginal Central Australians now presume the same type of participation from museums and their staff. I had this pointed out to me, in a slightly different way, after playing recordings of restricted initiation songs (held at the Melbourne Museum) to men in the community of Laramba (Napperby). It was a dark night, and the glow from the firelight only partially revealed people's expressions, but, as the songs played, I could hear the men talking quietly among themselves about how many of these songs should never have been recorded because they are too secretive. When asked what should be done with these recordings, one man replied, '[g]ive them to a *warlparl* [whitefella] to look after. Aboriginal people in town can't be trusted with these things. They're too dangerous'.

In other parts of Australia, however, Aboriginal communities will have quite different ideas and expectations. The type of complementary affiliation, and its possible extension to the museum, is likely not to apply to other groups where relationships between place, people, and objects vary. People will also have very different conceptions of individual and/or collective cultural property and have different experiences of collecting and collectors. Museums, therefore, need to open spaces for dialogue with people from different Indigenous communities and work with ideas that challenge existing dominant, academic, bureaucratic, and legalistic frameworks. The somewhat symbiotic model of care being proposed by Central Australian men, while not readily aligning with liberal sociopolitical agendas of 'self-determination', does nonetheless urge museum professionals to work in the messy and often complicated intercultural worlds of Central Australian Aboriginal people. It also demands ongoing dialogue with the owners of cultural collections. Decolonial museology is not straightforward to implement, as museums tend to have vast collections of objects sourced from a spatially dispersed and linguistically diverse range of peoples. At the same time, such museums may be situated within Indigenous communities that are themselves diverse, requiring decisions about who has representational legitimacy. Rather than retreating to idealised conceptions of Indigenous peoples or politicised rhetoric, such as 'decolonisation', the proposition presented here suggests a pivot towards greater attentiveness to different epistemological and ontological frameworks. It also elevates localised forms of governance around the cultural property. Responding to this will require resisting any tendency to pan-Aboriginalise the handling of these collections and instead work directly with those who have acquired knowledge of, and rights to, express knowledge about collections and their futures in accordance with specific Indigenous values, frameworks, and expectations.

## Spatial Reorganisation

A sincere engagement with this ontological diversity must, however, go beyond mere acknowledgement and recognition. Much of the literature around decolonisation has tended to emphasise forms of acknowledgement, expose injustices, and acknowledge the historical colonial contingencies under which collections were assembled (Kreps 2011, p. 72). There has been a tendency to identify and reveal these traits as a first step on the way to acknowledging diverse voices and perspectives. If these moves are to be anything more than an acknowledgement of the ravages of colonialism, however, then structural relations need to be altered and changes to practice made. One of the domains in which changes have been made to the handling of Australian Indigenous collections in recent years is the reorganisation of museum stores. As briefly touched on earlier, some museums have attempted to reorganise their collection stores so that objects that were once arranged by classic museum classifications, such as object type and size, are now regrouped following Indigenous perspectives.

As briefly mentioned earlier, some of these measures have already been piloted by the Strehlow Research Centre in Alice Springs but could also be trialled and adopted by other, much larger Australian museums. It is true that, being a smaller collection with extremely detailed collection documentation and descendent communities living nearby to guide its management, these types of initiatives have been much easier to implement (as per McCarthy's similar observations). Thanks to the interventions of anthropologists and Arrernte staff who wanted to make community consultations more efficient and 'safer' for people wanting to only interact with objects that they had specific rights to, a rehousing and reorganising project was undertaken. Objects relating to specific estates or those used in certain ceremonies, for example, were boxed together and kept near each other at the request of elders. Residing nearby or adjacent to each other in sealed boxes, and not distributed throughout a museum store according to Western forms of classifications, these objects now retain something of their pre-collection lives. These boxes are also labelled with the names of key ancestral sites and ancestors, making it easy to make connections with related manuscripts and audio–visual parts of the collection. Having conducted visits to these stores prior to this reorganisation and witnessing people's discomfort at not knowing what they might be exposed to, this space has been transformed into a place of cultural safety. Museum staff, Aboriginal and non-Aboriginal, also find this arrangement fruitful as the Indigenous cultural values of the objects, particularly the inherent links between objects, places, and generations of people, are made immediately evident. Older museum object typologies become quickly irrelevant. It is now a place where people can converse with their ancestors in physical form, engage in reflective group discussions, and ponder futures without fear of inadvertently transgressing into other people's cultural territory.

The reorganisation of collections along these lines can, nonetheless, present significant storage challenges as the physical dimensions of the gathered objects will be variable. Other Australian museums have for this reason avoided making such changes, given the staffing and resourcing requirements of moving, rehousing, relabelling, and then storing objects of dissimilar dimensions. Changes to the way Indigenous-restricted collections were physically managed, however, were undertaken decades earlier in most Australian museums, and should serve as an example of what can be achieved. I discussed these changes with the Melbourne Museums' curator of anthropology between 1967 and 1986, Mr. Alan West, and he reflected upon how internal museum decision-making gradually came to make these changes throughout the early 1970s:

> We had no one asking for access to restricted parts of the collection apart from scholars. At that stage there was almost no interest from the local Victorian Aboriginal people for access to the collections. I mean the Museum just wasn't in their vision at all . . . there was no decision, made by the Museum Board, or by the Director. These decisions were entirely the responsibility of the people of the curatorial staff.[1]

The decision to move restricted Indigenous collections to new storage locations accessible only to a limited number of approved staff reflected a growing realisation that change was needed. In subsequent decades, the museum developed policies about the handling, storage, and display of these objects, and they were later grouped according to cultural and linguistic regions. Considerable work has since gone into further reorganising this material so that objects are grouped according to specific cultural groups.

The question of the arrangement of the Melbourne Museum's Indigenous collections is not something well known. Excluding the very large items, the entire collection has now been deliberately and curatorially organised into

1 Personal Communication with Alan West 2/11/2012.

different Indigenous cultural groupings, across the main Australian Indigenous store, the related restricted collections store, and the Pacific collections. This strategy was implemented during the relocation of the collections to the new Melbourne Museum and its off-site store during the late 1990s. This physical relocation gave museum curatorial and collections staff an opportunity to dismantle the historical type-based storage arrangements and replace them with a layout that better reflected Indigenous expectations and values. One of the curators instrumental in making these changes, Lindy Allen, describes the motivation for making these changes:

> Our concern was that we were all aware and had witnessed the distress community members felt moving across the store to different areas, seeing their material sitting with that of other people's material, and feeling compromised and at times frightened by seeing material belonging to others, and for which they had no permissions or protections. It was revolutionary for the time – late 1990s – and the development of the Museum for the American Indian was happening at the same time and was impressed with this approach and influenced decisions.[2]

This philosophical approach was consistently applied to all areas – exhibitions, collection relocation, and collection storage layout. Under a curatorial team led by Indigenous curator Gaye Sculthorpe, everything was considered through the prism of the rights and interests of Indigenous people. Once the collections arrived at their new storage sites, they were reorganised into 'cultural groupings' based on a combination of geographic and cultural associations. Each curator with expertise in different parts of Indigenous Australia – for example, northern, central, and southeast – had responsibility for working their way through the collections, drilling down into the provenance history of objects to construct new groupings that made sense both historically and to contemporary communities. Some groups were organised at a finer level of detail. For instance, the Yolngu material from Yirrkala that came from collector Donald Thomson, who produced detailed documentation like that produced by T. G. H. Strehlow, could be further broken down into clans. These 'storage groups' were also replicated in the collections database, and each object had to be allocated to a 'group' by the curator. Other changes were made at times at the request of communities. Allen has, for example, written about the Lamalama people's request that their material is re-grouped as it was originally placed adjacent to West Cape York material, people they considered enemies or at least 'unknowns' (Allen & Hamby 2011). Ultimately, the intention was to create a flow through the storeroom that gave a sense of moving across the continent, country by country, in the arrangement of the collection on shelves or in cabinets across the stores.

2 Personal Communication with Lindy Allen 24/02/2022.

The spatial reorganisation of collecting institutions in response to community needs is not an insignificant matter. A museum environment that better accommodates Indigenous research and elevates Indigenous conceptions of cultural heritage will necessarily reflect this in its physical design. In the examples discussed earlier, the initial *acknowledgement* that cultural affiliations, with their distinct relationships to land and place, are the source of Indigenous knowledge and led to concrete changes to the way objects were handled and classified. Such changes came about via Indigenous people's long-term engagements with their cultural patrimony, greater inclusion of Indigenous staff, and willingness from institutions to respond. Future refinements in storage, access, and handling will only emerge via continued dialogue and a deepening of these relationships with a view to physically transform the pragmatic structures of institutions.

## Conclusion: *Mwanty-irreme*, to Proceed with Care

All these collaborative transformations, and many more, are most likely to flourish when collecting institutions move away from older models of possession and preservation towards new paradigms of care. This is not to suggest that collecting institutions have not been careful with their collections because they undoubtedly have been, but there ought to be a new emphasis on supporting contemporary engagements. An emphasis on care focused on the provision of what is necessary for the health, welfare, maintenance, and nurturance of people and things, whereas preservation tends to promote stasis, containment, possession, and the maintenance of things in their original or existing state. The emphasis on care need not, however, be an affront to the ideology of museums in general. On the contrary, museums have long operated under the assumption that their collections possess not only historical value but opportunities for present use and yet unknown future potentials. The challenge for museums, however, is to maintain the integrity of their collections while, at the same, allowing them to be transformed through acts of return and repatriation, as well as emergent forms of management and handling.

Therefore, these transformations may come slowly, via 'careful' collaborations. Arrernte elders have repeatedly stressed, for example, the need to '*mwanty-irreme*', to be careful, or, perhaps more precisely, to proceed deliberately but with caution. Visiting the stores of the South Australian Museum in early 2022, I sent photos of ceremonial shields painted with different ancestral and totemic designs via text message to my Anmatyerr co-researchers (who were unable to join me on a research visit due to the COVID-19 pandemic). Discussing these images later with elders again reminded me that the only way to proceed with sharing these designs was slowly. They needed time to identify the right families that might be responsible for these designs or be related to the original makers. They wanted to make sure that information associated with the objects (that was held by the museum) was revealed in the right contexts. They needed time to pre-empt how this return might potentially affect contemporary understandings of relationships between people, land, and ancestors. Source communities in other parts of the world are similarly making calls for the need 'to talk about the re-contextualisation' before return occurs as these objects enter into 'new contexts' and, thus, 'serve new purposes' (Hassan-Bello in Onabolu 2022).

The Arrernte reminder to *mwanty-irreme* might, therefore, be seen as an argument for conceptual space to rethink and reorganise an improved cultural heritage infrastructure – one that emerges out of the advances made in recent decades around the development of local infrastructure, the recruitment of Indigenous staff, internships, co-designed research projects, and further capacity building. Institutions grounded in care might also inaugurate new types of heritage infrastructures that are based not on benevolence or generosity but on equity and justice.

## Note

1 https://twitter.com/sirma_bilge/status/1482554411213897730.

## References

Allen, L. & Hamby, L. 2011, 'Pathways to Knowledge: Research, Agency and Power Relations in the Context of Collaborations Between Museums and Source Communities', in S. Byrne, R. Torrence, A. Clarke, & R. Harrison (eds), *Unpacking the Collection: Networks of Material and Social Agency in the Museum*, Springer, New York, pp. 209–229.

Andrews, J. 2022, 'Value Creation and Museums from an Indigenous Perspective', in H. Morphy & R. McKenzie (eds), *Museums, Societies and the Creation of Value*, Routledge, London, pp. 225–239.

Betts, R. 2012, 'Decolonization: A Brief History of the Word', in E. Bogaerts & R. Raben (eds), *Beyond Empire and Nation: The Decolonization of African and Asian Societies, 1930s–1970s*, Brill, Leiden, pp. 23–38.

Bignall, S. 2010, *Postcolonial Agency: Critique and Constructivism*, Edinburgh University Press, Edinburgh.

Bignall, S. 2014, 'The Collaborative Struggle for Excolonialism', *Settler Colonial Studies,* vol. 4, no. 4, pp. 340–356, Routledge, https://doi.org/10.1080/2201473X.2014.911651.

Bolton, L. 2001, 'The Object in View: Aborigines, Melanesians, and Museums', in A. Rumsey & J. Weiner (eds), *Emplaced Myth: Space, Narrative, and Knowledge in Aboriginal Australia and Papua New Guinea*, University of Hawai'i Press, Honolulu, pp. 215–232, https://doi.org/10.2307/j.ctvvn7zh.14.

Brus, A. & Zillinger, M. 2021, 'Introduction: Transforming the Post/Colonial Museum', *Zeitschrift für Kulturwissenschaften*, vol. 15, no. 2 (December 1, 2021), pp. 11–28, https://doi.org/10.14361/zfk-2021-150203.

Butler, D. 2022, 'Gweagal Descendants Given Private Viewing of Spears Taken by Captain Cook', *NITV*, April 6, accessed May 23, 2022, from www.sbs.com.au/nitv/article/2022/04/06/gweagal-descendants-given-private-viewing-spears-taken-captain-cook-1.

Chakrabarty, D. 2000, *Provincializing Europe: Postcolonial Thought and Historical Difference*, Princeton University Press, Princeton, NJ.

Chalmers, J. 2017, 'The Transformation of Academic Knowledges: Understanding the Relationship between Decolonising and Indigenous Research Methodologies', *Socialist Studies/Études Socialistes,* vol. 12, no. 1, pp. 97–97, https://doi.org/10.18740/S4GH0C.

Clifford, J. 1997, 'Museums as Contact Zones', in *Routes: Travel and Translation in the Late Twentieth Century*, Harvard University Press, Cambridge, MA, pp. 188–219.

Clifford, J. 2001, 'Indigenous Articulations'. *The Contemporary Pacific,* vol. 13, no. 2, pp. 468–490.

Clifford, J. 2013, *Returns: Becoming Indigenous in the Twenty First Century*, Harvard University Press, Cambridge, MA.

Clifford, J. & Marcus, G. (eds) 1986, *Writing Culture: The Poetics and Politics of Ethnography: A School of American Research Advanced Seminar*, University of California Press, Berkeley.

Coombes, A.E. & Phillips, R.B. (eds.) 2020, *Museum Transformations: Decolonization and Democratization.* John Wiley & Sons, West Sussex.

CRANAplus. 2021, *First Peoples Strategy,* Museums Victoria, Melbourne.

Desmond, M. 2014, 'Relational Ethnography', *Theory and Society,* vol. 43, no. 5, pp. 547–579, https://doi.org/10.1007/s11186-014-9232-5.

Foley, G. 2002, 'How Indigenous People Have Altered the Function of the Melbourne Museum', Unpublished Manuscripts, pp. 1–14.

Gibson, J. 2019, '"You're My Kwertengerl": Transforming Models of Care for Central Australian Aboriginal Museum Collections', *Museum Management and Curatorship,* vol. 34, no. 3, pp. 240–256, https://doi.org/10.1080/09647775.2018.1549506.

Gibson, J. 2020, *Ceremony Men: Making Ethnography and the Return of the Strehlow Collection,* SUNY Press, Albany NY.

Hymes, D. 1972, *Reinventing Anthropology*, 1st ed., Pantheon Books, New York.

Johnston, I.G., Meara, T., Ley, L., Simpson, C., Lyons, J., Rutherford, R. & Quadri, D. 2021, 'The AIATSIS Return of Cultural Heritage Project: Understanding Aboriginal and Torres Strait Islander Cultural Heritage Material Held Overseas and the Initial Challenges to Repatriating Material to Custodians', *Curator: The Museum Journal,* vol. 64, no. 4, pp. 653–674, https://doi.org/10.1111/cura.12440.

Kreps, C. 2011, 'Changing the Rules of the Road: Postcolonialism and the New Ethics of Museum Anthropology', in J. Marstine (ed), *The Routledge Companion to Museum Ethics: Redefining Ethics for the Twenty-First-Century Museum*, Routledge, London and New York, pp. 70–85.

Krmpotich, C. & Peers, L. 2013, *This Is Our Life: Haida Material Heritage and Changing Museum Practice*, University of British Columbia Press, Vancouver.

Krouse, S. 2006, 'Anthropology and the New Museology', *Reviews in Anthropology,* vol. 35, no. 2, pp. 169–182, https://doi.org/10.1080/00938150600698336.

McCarthy, C. 2011, *Museums and Māori: Heritage Professionals, Indigenous Collections, Current Practice*, Taylor & Francis Group, Milton, UK.

Merlan, F. 2006, 'Beyond Tradition', *The Asia Pacific Journal of Anthropology,* vol. 7, no. 1, pp. 85–104, https://doi.org/10.1080/14442210600554507.

Modest, W. 2019, 'Introduction: Ethnographic Museums and the Double Bind', in W. Modest, N. Thomas, & D. Prlić (eds), *Matters of Belonging: Ethnographic Museums in a Changing Europe*, Sidestone Press, Leiden, pp. 9–22.

Morphy, H. 2015, 'Open Access Versus the Culture of Protocols', in R. Silverman (ed), *Museum as Process: Translating Local and Global Knowledges*, Routledge, New York, pp. 90–104.

Myers, F.R. 1986, *Pintupi Country, Pintupi Self: Sentiment, Place and Politics Among Western Desert Aborigines*, University of California Press, Berkley.

Myers, F.R. 2017, 'Exhibiting Culture at the Boundary: The Fetish of Early Papunya Boards', in L. Scholes (ed), *Tjungunutja: From Having Come Together*, Museum and Art Gallery of the Northern Territory, Darwin, pp. 2–13.

Neale, T. in press, 'What Tradition Affords: Articulations of Indigeneity in Contemporary Bushfire Management'. *Current Anthropology*.

Office for the Arts. n.d., *International Repatriation Highlights*, Department of Infrastructure, Transport, Regional Development and Communications, accessed October 20, 2021, from www.arts.gov.au/what-we-do/cultural-heritage/indigenous-repatriation/international-repatriation/recent-international.

Onabolu, T. 2022, 'As 26 Looted Treasure Go on View in Benin Republic, the West African Cultural Community Is Asking: What Happens Next?' *Artnet*, March 11, accessed May 22, 2022, from https://news.artnet.com/art-world/benin-republic-restitution-2083328.

Pawu-Kurlpurlurnu, W.J., Holmes, M. & Box, A. 2008, *Ngurra-Kurlu: A Way of Working with Warlpiri People*. Desert Knowledge Cooperative Research Centre 41, Desert Knowledge CRC, Alice Springs, accessed May 22, 2022, from https://www.nintione.com.au/resource/DKCRC-Report-41-Ngurra-kurlu.pdf.

Phillips, R.B. 2005, 'Re-Placing Objects: Historical Practices for the Second Museum Age', *The Canadian Historical Review,* vol. 86, no. 1, pp. 83–110, https://doi.org/10.1353/can.2005.0086.

Phillips, R.B. 2011, *Museum Pieces: Toward the Indigenization of Canadian Museums,* McGill-Queen's University Press, Montréal.

Stanton, J. 2011, 'Ethnographic Museums and Collections: From the Past into the Future', in L. Paroissien & D. Griffin (eds), *Understanding Museums: Australian Museums and Museology*, National Museum of Australia, Canberra, accessed May 22, 2022, from https://nma.gov.au/research/understanding-museums/JStanton_2011.html.

Wergin, C. 2021, 'Healing through Heritage?: The Repatriation of Human Remains from European Collections as Potential Sites of Reconciliation', *Anthropological Journal of European Cultures*, vol. 30, no. 1 (March 1, 2021), pp. 123–133, https://doi.org/10.3167/ajec.2021.300109.

# 6 Conclusion

## Reflections on Return

I recall sitting cross-legged on the Ti Tree community football oval lawn with a group of Anmatyerr men in 2006. I was present as a bystander when consultants from a major Australian museum came through the community to discuss the potential repatriation of secret-sacred objects. Anmatyerr men sat in five or six separate groups, in accordance with their different relationships to country and kin, and listened intently as extracts from collection documentation were read out, and images of the objects were shared among the assembled group. The process was slightly awkward as the consultant's clumsy pronunciation of Anmatyerr place names and totems caused some confusion, and the group waited quietly for each object record to be read out. Once printouts of the documentation were in their hands, however, younger Anmatyerr men stepped forward to read these written descriptions and convert the poorly written renderings of their language into something recognisable to Anmatyerr speakers. Given that these collections were reasonably well documented and the assembled men possessed excellent knowledge of their local Dreamings and cultural traditions, most of these objects were eventually linked to either a person or estate group that could take repossession of them.

A few months later, I was out travelling with many of these same men on a hunting expedition when our road was unexpectedly blocked by a swelling creek that had come up after significant rains. Deciding to set up 'dinner camp' and wait for the waters to recede, we lit a fire to cook a kangaroo and chatted while we waited. The eldest man who belonged to a faction within the community that identified more strongly with families from the west and who spoke both Warlpiri and Anmatyerr began to talk about the cache of objects that had been repatriated to him by the museum. Men from his cohort were pleased that the return had occurred and agreed that the objects should stay with this elder in recognition of his cultural expertise. Men from the other group, however, who identified more closely with Anmatyerr-speaking families in the east, appeared less comfortable. They asked probing questions. Precisely whose traditional lands and Dreamings did these objects related to? Why had not they been asked to share in the custodianship? Where were these objects now? Discovering that many of the objects once belonged to

DOI: 10.4324/9781003158752-6

their fathers and grandfathers, and were, thus, considered their rightful and inheritance, the eastern men were clearly offended. Looking visibly upset and agitated, one of these men stated the repatriated collections needed to be 'repatriated again' and redistributed according to family associations and not according to cultural seniority. In his view, the museum had not understood the way these objects were properly conveyed across generations via patrilineal lines, and the western men had taken advantage of this ignorance to bolster their position as cultural experts at the expense of others. The well-intentioned repatriation of these objects had exacerbated existing conflicts between families and groups.

It was this experience that first alerted me to the, often unseen, issues that communities faced when cultural collections came home. Since then, I have worked alongside numerous Aboriginal communities in Central Australia and in partnership with many different collecting institutions to advance best-practice cultural heritage returns and better understand these challenges. Being an active participant in endeavours to help Indigenous communities re-engage with collections has been an extremely rewarding experience, but, beyond this, I think that it has helped all involved rethink complex pasts and imagine new positive futures. The central aim of this book has been to convey some of these experiences so that an evidence-based, ethnographically informed approach might be used to inform the development of future collecting institutions and source community engagements. Moving beyond postcolonial critiques of collections that tend to cast them as instruments of 'collecting, ordering, and governing' (Bennett et al. 2017), my aim has been instead to bring to the fore the way these collections are being re-engaged with and the expectations that different cohorts – in collecting institutions, among researchers, and in the different source communities – have of them. In doing so, I have attempted to explore the fields of meaning and value creation, as people (Indigenous and non-Indigenous) interrogate, critique, rediscover, and perform/play with returned collections.

In this concluding chapter, I come back to the rhetoric of repatriation and match this against some of these expectations. In particular cases, there is no doubt that the repatriation of physical objects will, and has been, be the best outcome. It is not, however, the major issue facing collections and archives at present. As this book shows, there will always be difficult issues of how and to whom material is to be returned, how stakeholder communities are defined, and how they might be best resourced to incorporate repatriated materials back into their future lives. In Central Australia, a great deal of secret-sacred collections have already been repatriated from domestic institutions, and international museums are increasingly entering into dialogue (Johnston et al. 2021), but the questions now are how and to whom other types of material might be returned, how those communities could be better resourced to incorporate this repatriated material, and whether repatriation is indeed their priority. It needs to be noted, however, that the number of requests for the physical repatriation of cultural objects from these communities has been very small compared with the size of the numerous collections made. Furthermore, communities are rarely, if ever, asked to have original analogue recordings or photographic materials repatriated as digital copies provide better quality materials that can be distributed more easily. Writing about the fate of ethnographic collections in Germany, Glenn Penny has concluded that '[t]he question that should concern us is not repatriation yes or no, but what should be done with these collections? Repatriation is only one small part of the answer' (Penny 2021, p. 199). A central problem with public debates about these collections and repatriation today, he goes on, is that 'no one discusses the uncontroversial objects, their hidden histories, and their great potential' (Penny 2021, p. 196). As the experiences given here illustrate, the potential of these collections can only ever be realised once understood outside of the archive and placed within a terrain of practical activity, where they take on extraordinary existential value.

## Interculturality

The labour and performativity of return is profoundly intercultural. The concept of the intercultural has been applied to Indigenous collecting and collections elsewhere (Jonaitis & Glass 2010) and can help us think about the dynamic processes of cultural contact, social exchange, and relations of mediation that occur between groups of people. This perspective posits that the objectification of Indigenous cultural heritage is shared (albeit unevenly) by Indigenous people and settler-colonists, and this process is contested at every stage. This is especially so as Indigenous cultural heritage collections continue to circulate between and across varying sociocultural domains and though differing regimes of value. None of this refutes Indigenous claims to this material but places the work of returning, reintegrating, caring for, and recirculating cultural collections beyond the binary. While this approach comes with its own set of challenges, it acknowledges the relational and processual nature of social reality and urges us to think about boundaries rather than bounded groups and cultural conflict rather than group culture. As Bourdieu (in Merlan 2005, p. 179) has observed, when people come together (even, or perhaps especially, in contrasting or conflictual ways), it is not enough to explain each point of view separately. Interaction has an inherent polyvalence about it: no single perspective will account for what happens. If nothing else, this book makes an argument for an intercultural appreciation of Indigenous cultural heritage collections and their afterlives.

The global movements for Indigenous cultural restitution, often led by activists, have focused on the issues of ownership, control, and sovereignty. From this perspective, notions of 'shared stewardship' can be criticised for overriding painful pasts and negating Indigenous moves towards self-determination. Similarly, analyses that emphasise entanglement and complexity have been criticised for avoiding the realities of colonial violence and the need for 'cultural restitution' (Hicks 2020, pp. 25–36). It is true that museums have in some cases taken refuge behind notions of complexity and dialogue as ways of avoiding the difficult work of returning Indigenous collections, but, as the examples in this book illustrate, there have been considerable advancements made in recent decades. Notions of re-engagement, return, value creation (Morphy & McKenzie 2021), and re-entanglement (Basu 2021) also continue to be guiding themes emerging from the history of ethnographic collections and the work currently being done on them by and with their stakeholder communities.

Calls to 'repatriate everything', however, principled in white anti-racist discourse and amplified in the popular media, often fail to acknowledge the realities of cultural heritage return that I have detailed in this short book. Most assume that it is known to whom things should be returned to and rarely consider how this might occur or the complexities of ownership. The simplistic view of returning items to a 'country' (see Chapter 3) also overlooks the at times contested nature of land tenure and its relationship to cultural heritage. Moreover, the examples given here demonstrate that few inhabitants of Central Australian Aboriginal communities demand complete independence from Western cultural heritage institutions and the dominant Euro-Australia society more broadly. Their view of the situation is often the complete opposite: the non-Aboriginal population, in the form of government services and resourcing, has to step up to its obligations (Peterson 2022, p. 10). In the context of using cultural heritage collections then, there is an expectation from communities that these institutions will work for Aboriginal interests. Once the great accumulators of ethnographica for collecting institutions, curators and researchers are also now increasingly taking objects back to the sites where they were originally collected. As several people experienced in the return have acknowledged, in many of these circumstances, it is often 'non-Aboriginal people working in cultural institutions', who are most anxious about seeing objects returned (Galt-Smith 2001). This modern, intercultural 'ritual' of return (Peers, Reinius & Shannon 2017; Batty 2006), therefore, offers not just opportunities for Indigenous recipients but, perhaps, even partial redemption for settler-colonial society too.

The return of objects is also not always the priority, and issues of representation may feature just as highly. The representation of Indigenous people with collections and exhibitions is a contested and complex space. Indigenous people use these representations to establish the terms of their recognition as a distinct people, but they also understand that these same objectifications can promulgate alienated versions of themselves. Glass writes of a 'simultaneous reliance on and mistrust of' objectified cultural collections and descriptions made by outsiders (Glass 2021, p. 17). Chapter 2 illustrates some of the ways that Central Australian Aboriginal people grapple with the tentacular nature of anthropological forms of representation and have begun to re-appropriate these materials to inspire their telling of history, through often personal connections to the past. Museum objects, audio–visual recordings, and other data are being actively used to create exciting new forms of self-representation, self-expression, and innovation.

European museums concerned with colonial restitution have slightly different concerns. They deal with source communities beyond their borders and in states that were once their colonies. In settler-colonial contexts, however, we are dealing with very different dynamics, whereby the return of cultural collections can be used as a way of rectifying historical injustices within a shared society. In Chapter 5, I examine how different decolonial moves are employed as ways of reframing the ongoing workings of coloniality in the present. The experiences of return discussed throughout this book reveal unanticipated responses, awkward encounters, cross-cultural tensions, and anxieties, which ought to ultimately help us rethink new cultural heritage infrastructures. As much as museums in Australia are increasingly committed to conversations about the return, there is still much more work to be done. Where collections are returned in ways most suitable to the relevant stakeholders, a new space of dialogue has developed, and as international examples of repatriation have also shown, these experiences can unite people 'across spatial borders and heritage temporalities' (Wergin 2021, p. 131). As described in Chapter 4, these long overdue moves to see communities reconnected with cultural heritage collections may even lead to the types of Indigenous-led 'new collecting'. Similarly, the return of ancestral remains – which, like the return of secret-sacred objects, has progressed enormously in Australia since the 1970s – has seen some Aboriginal communities now happy to participate in using 'ancestor's bones' to learn about the deep past (Turnbull 2017, p. 364). The perquisite, of course, is that senior men and women co-design and supervise these projects to ensure that benefits are returned to their communities.

## Collected-Repatriated-Stolen-Returned Again

In November 2020, I received an email alerting me to an unusual story. The email had been sent by an Aboriginal person whose friend had discovered a cache of Central Australian sacred objects in a private collection, 2,700 km away from their home, in Gippsland Victoria. Written on the objects in the black pen were museum accession numbers and annotations that identified their associated totems and other information. Looking into the history of these objects, I discovered that they had been collected from Anmatyerr men between 1927 and 1932 and had been then either sold or donated to the museum, where they stayed until they were repatriated as part of the event described earlier in 2008. Once back in the community, most of these objects – which were part of a different set to those mentioned earlier – had been handed over to the son of the man that had originally traded them. This elderly man took these objects to his remote outstation, and for the next six years, they were kept in a secretive location and revealed only to men at annual initiation ceremonies. Lacking the facilities needed to store collections like this safely, however, the elderly man had decided to keep his cache in the boot of a broken-down car on the edge of his community, away from the comings and goings of everyday life. Caring for these objects in a way that seemed softest, he took control of his cultural belongings and used the resources available to him to find a solution. The constraints of poverty and the fact that his traditional lands had been annexed by pastoralism in the mid-twentieth century, however, mean that his options were limited. Despite these best efforts, six years later, this vulnerable cache of repatriated objects was eventually discovered by a non-Indigenous building contractor and stolen.

The rediscovering of these repatriated-then-stolen objects tells us much about object values, their vulnerabilities, and their movement and circulation across time and space. Objects that were valued in their local Aboriginal religious contexts and handed between individuals and groups for many years (possibly hundreds of years for wooden objects and possibly longer for stone objects?) became objects of aesthetic and anthropological curiosity with the arrival of settler-colonialism and acceptance of the 'dissolution of native societies' (Wolfe 2006, p. 388). The objects in question, collected by an anthropologist and a missionary, were not taken coercively; however, the conditions of their giving were far from equal. From this point on, the communities that knew these objects both lamented their absence but also replaced them or adjusted accordingly. Their arrival back in the community nearly 80 years later via the museum's repatriation project, though welcomed, required further readjustments, and the fact that they were soon after stolen indicates just how tenuous this re-integration can be. As I was later involved in seeing these once traded/collected, then stolen objects returned yet again to these communities, I could not help wondering if they might be welcomed back into the ongoing religious lives of the Anmatyerr people. The objects were handed over at a meeting of senior men who expressed surprise that they had been stolen. Many assumed that they had been taken by other kin and were in circulation among other communities. When I later visited the relevant community a year later, I was taken to many of the key sites that these objects related to as a way of showing how, even in their absence, first since the 1920s–1930s and then again between 2014 and 2021, the knowledge, songs, stories, and ceremonies that these objects denoted continued to have currency.

In the introductory chapter, I noted that, as more and more communities lobby for access, enter museums, and engage with the histories of their collections, the trajectories of these objects and collections – through time and place – come into view. While this movement is generally presented as a unidirectional transaction, whereby cultural objects are first taken and then returned, the reality is often far more complex. We are better served conceiving of these movements as trajectories, involving multifaceted relationships between people, institutions, places, and ancestors, rather than as episodic transactions. As Chapters 2 and 4 demonstrate, the often-complicated histories that communities have had with different collectors in the past and their current concerns about some objects returning, especially where capacities to make confident decisions about custodianship/ownership are strained, will each play a role in these object trajectories. These objects do not necessarily move along linear trajectories back to their communities but may stay where they are, be loaned, copied, or be augmented by having community input put back into collection documentation.

## Struggles and Challenges

The social and cultural labours of re-integrating collections have also been a theme of this book. Whether returned as digital audio–visual copies, printed materials, or physical objects, the re-introduction of these materials into changed and changing social and ecological landscapes can unsettle, disturb, and/or provoke. In these societies where responsibility for cultural knowledge and material is typically invested in individuals and their close kin (as defined by dreaming and country relationships), taking collective or communal control over returned collections presents difficulties. This is made doubly tricky as most communities in Central Australia lack the reliable cultural heritage facilities needed to support this approach to collective custodianship, such as a museum, an archive, or a keeping place. These issues, while certainly pronounced in Central Australia, do, nevertheless, arise in other Indigenous contexts. In her analysis of the 'fates repatriated objects' among the Native American Makah communities in the Pacific Northwest, Anne Tweedie (2002) has, for example, commented on how people fret over the safety of objects repatriated through the North American Graves Protection and Repatriation Act. Central Australian Aboriginal peoples, such as the Makah, have also found it challenging to reconcile new forms of 'community' ownership with the more classical models of family and individual possession (Tweedie 2002, p. 122). What Tweedie describes as a 'struggle' to manage returned collections; I describe as experiments in re-integration. In both cases, communal forms of ownership are imagined as likely working best through the establishment of local museums or keeping places; however, it is ironic that this model encourages communities to act in ways that are often counter to their everyday, contemporary practices.

The lack of cultural heritage services and facilities in Central Australia, coupled with the feelings of cultural endangerment discussed in Chapter 4, means that museums are being sought out reservoirs of cultural material and sites of cultural activity. As Anmatyerr man Martin Hagan has commented in relation to his community's desires for the future:

> We want everything back in local museums in our communities. But for now, there are no reliable, safe places to do this. With the old

people's permission, the objects, recordings, and notes made as part of our Anmatyerr shields project need go to a good museum.

Reiterating Anmatyerr people's inalienable rights to these cultural materials and that they need to be free to circulate back to Anmatyerr people, a 'good museum' in his estimation is 'a place where they'll be safe until a time that they might come back'. Hagan's comments are suggestive of the larger themes of relationality and passage that permeate through this text. As diverse collections, including objects, copies of audio–visual materials, manuscripts, and photographs, have re-entered Anmatyerr and Arrernte communities for many years now, there is an acknowledgement that collecting institutions need not be an endpoint, but a node in a series of unending exchanges. Put simply, objects can move in and out of different contexts and where they do; they are, perhaps, more appropriately being acknowledged as alive.

Many of the examples given in this book centre upon the experience of the Arrernte people who are arguably the most documented Aboriginal group in Australia. Since the late 1800s, their language has been closely documented, their material culture avidly collected, and their ceremonial and religious practices documented in extensive audio–visual form. Though the Arrernte case is extreme, this ethnographic attention makes them prime exemplars of the modern predicament of Indigenous peoples globally and the typically challenging status of cultural (often anthropological) collections and information among them. Aaron Glass's numerous writings on Kwakwaka'wakw people's long and detailed engagements with collectors, anthropologists, and museum collections have some important parallels (Glass 2021, 2018, 2014). As his work also testifies, these Indigenous collections often upset the neat boundaries of decolonising discourse because of their co-production within colonial and Indigenous lifeworlds. On the one hand, Indigenous people rely on these representations to establish the terms of their recognition as sovereign and distinct peoples, but, on the other hand, these representations can promulgate estranged versions of themselves (Glass 2021, p. 17). The return of collections can, therefore, at times produce awkward and hesitant interactions when the historical versions of themselves present as discordant with contemporary life experiences. Deciding what to do with recordings of ceremonial songs that have been out of circulation for many years (Chapter 4) or objects that no longer have a comfortable home (Chapter 3) can invoke melancholic, strained, and unresolved reactions. There are important questions that need to be asked in terms of not only 'who' collections might be returned to, but to 'where'. Ascertaining where collections go, is important in both in terms of contested claims to land as well as the more practical concerns of to what facility? At the same time, this movement of cultural heritage back into the social lives of people today has generated opportunities for building new forms of self-representation and local identity formations.

As discussed in Chapter 4, in some cases, better access to collections and interactions with collecting institutions are leading to experimentation with 'new collecting'. Whether this will become a feature of these transforming museums and source community relations is unknown; nonetheless, it heralds the continuing relevancy of the collecting institutions for Indigenous communities. These relationships do not necessarily challenge the push for local cultural centres and keeping places but rather provide an alternate avenue for communities that either lack adequate cultural heritage resourcing, are unable to prioritise this work, or would also like to develop partnerships of mutual obligation beyond their communities. These experiences also remind us that digital return has been an incredibly successful method because people have been able to make informed choices about their collections. People can know where things are, carry out their own independent research, and/or build relations with collecting institutions if desired.

## Knowledge Making

Re-engagements with these collections have not been wholly about contemporary desires, intentions, and uses; part of the labour of return has required a better understanding of the history of how ethnographic collections are made. People are not just interested in the contents of these collections but also in how they came into being, the relationships between collectors and informants, and the way museums have cared for and displayed them. The dynamic ways that Warumungu, Arrernte, and Anmatyerr people have responded to various anthropological collections (Chapters 2 and 4) illustrate their interest in these histories and finding ways to respond to them. Understanding the affordances of these materials for contemporary and future generations requires knowledge of the conditions and contexts of their making. While discovering the identities of individual makers for certain objects can be extremely difficult, especially among older collections, giving communities access to collection objects and their documentation can generate significant genealogical links to historical collecting. Making these links brings objects closer to contemporary life and helps unlock their potential to inspire.

Recognising Indigenous participation in the production and contemporary reception of these collections ought to influence the way we think about these materials. Taking Indigenous agency and encounters seriously, both in the histories and futures of these collections, encourages us to temper critiques of ethnographic assemblages as simple expressions of settler-colonialist dogma or reifying anthropological theory. The intercultural nature of the material not only changes the way we see the history of its production but informs current Indigenous projects and activities that are aimed at recuperating, recontextualising, or re-signifying this material towards their own ends. In contexts where collection objects now move through communities in different forms, people have been free to interrogate these histories and produce new knowledge. The artistic responses from people such as Joel Liddle and Joseph Williams have taken these collections and used them to create new analyses of colonial encounters. Rather than seeing these materials as sites of disempowerment, their access to the digitised collections of Spencer and Gillen has enabled a continuation of the agency and initiative shown by their Arrernte and Warumungu predecessors. Re-engagement with ethnographic collections from this purview has certainly re-centred Indigenous actors and added to the growing literature on their roles as brokers and agents (Glass 2006; Gibson 2022) but has also seen Indigenous people acknowledge and better understand the complex role of collectors. Another aim of the book has been to show how people will say very different things about coloniality according to the different contexts and histories. The examples from southeastern Australia were discussed in Chapter 3 where there were very specific engagements with nineteenth-century collectors such as Alfred Howitt, which contrasts with the experiences of say Anmatyerr and Arrernte people who worked with T. G. H. Strehlow in the mid-twentieth century. The manuscript materials collected by Howitt in Victoria and New South Wales, therefore, have a very different resonance with people in that region compared to the return of recordings of ceremonial songs to Anmatyerr communities.

I contend that these experiences show that Indigenous readings of these ethnographic collections put them at the forefront of innovative research on collection histories. These engagements show how the very 'knowledge' that these collections generate is continually constituted via complex, historically located relationships between people and things. They prompt us to go beyond the search for an Indigenous agency in the archive (Harrison, Byrne & Clarke 2013) but to discover the unequal, but mutually constituted, production of cultural knowledge. As Williams' adoption of the Warumungu concept *ngijinkirri* (described in Chapter 2) illustrates, there is enormous scope for a diversity of Indigenous philosophies, frameworks, and ideas to shape theory and scholarship in this domain. Elevating Indigenous concepts may, in fact, be more fruitful than relying too much on external theoretical, moral, or political positions.

## New Frontiers

The notion that objects can be simply 'put back' into their original cultural contexts, as discussed in Chapter 3, is an over-simplification. Writing about Indigenous perspectives in museum collections, the Yuwaalaraay scholar Jilda Andrews has noted that 'Indigenous engagements with these collections today are more than simply a re-culturation of this material back into Indigenous culture. They broach new frontiers' (Andrews 2017, p. 91). The case studies of what happens 'after the return' provided in this book lend further weight to Andrew's observation. Practices of re-engagement and return, which are fast becoming fundamental to 'best practice' in the Australian museum sector, are enabling Central Australian Aboriginal communities to harness objects in order to help better understand our collective histories and build new relationships. As these materials recirculate, a new chapter is opening before us where people can begin to see repatriation as one option among many and think deeply about who owns the future of these collections.

Under the continued spectre of cultural endangerment, people are as much concerned with present control and ownership of collections as they are about what those who follow might inherit. What value will they be able to add to the already large corpus of cultural material collected? How can long-term benefits in the future be imagined? As argued in Chapter 5, part of that thinking takes in the role of collecting institutions. How can these institutions function for Indigenous interests in the future? In some ways, this thinking is far more radical than requests to decolonise and have material physically repatriated. Wanting to be recognised as members of a common public and, thus, resist settler-colonial logics of elimination (Rowse & Smith 2010), cultural collections offer important opportunities. As explored throughout this book, people are using these re-engagements as ways to imagine new relationships and build transformative concepts and practices in the hope that they may better recognise and cater to Indigenous interests.

These re-engagements also produce new frontiers at the personal level. Being confronted with collections for the first time, it is not uncommon for people to ask questions such as 'what does this object want me to do?' 'What responsibilities and obligations do I have to this object?' 'What would my old people want me to act?' As an example, in 2021, an Australian Research Council linkage project involving the Berndt Museum, Deakin University, the South Australian Museum, and the Warlayirti and Warlukurlangu Aboriginal Art Centres facilitated the digitisation and return of the 800-colour crayon drawing produced by Aboriginal stockmen in 1945 and collected by the anthropologist Ronald M. Berndt. Seeing his grandfather Paddy Padoon's drawing for the first time, Jaru man Robert McKay Tjungarrayi described his response in this way. 'When I first saw the drawings . . . wow! I nearly cried. I got really emotional. We didn't go looking for this story. This story came looking for us'. Taking a moment to compose himself, MacKay continued by reflecting on how these drawings might influence the vital relationships to the country (as described in Chapter 3).

> I really thank old Paddy for those drawings because they have brought me here to find important places like Lirrangkani and Garrang-garrang. I feel like it's my job, and the job of other people now, to understand these drawings and use them to find special places that haven't been visited for a long time, to get the right people back here and try and understand them . . . In showing and giving Berndt all these drawings, I think Paddy kind of left a map for his grandsons. That's kind of what we have to follow you know. That map.

The rhetoric around Indigenous cultural collections is often too quick to see these objects through the lens of contemporary politics and social relations, and the overbearing rhetoric of repatriation can lead to a kind of paralysis that makes this exploratory work harder. McKay's response suggests that there also needs to be time to pause and reflect, to ponder the motivations and expectations of ancestors, and to consider one's responsibilities to both past and future generations. There is a need to conduct research, ask questions, wonder, and come to an understanding of the different potentialities, what Cate Massola (Forthcoming) refers to as the 'time and space' for people 'to (re)value their objects and potentially make new ones'. These processes, which may take unexpected detours and lead to unanticipated reactions, eventually lead to an object's journey 'home' – in whatever form that may take.

## Final Words

I hope that this book helps complexify discussions about the repatriation of Indigenous cultural heritage and reveals more about the various forms of 'return' that has taken place. People's interest and use of these collections are multiple and do not always centre on claims to repossess objects. To paraphrase cross-cultural historian Maria Nugent, 'the return' that people get '*from* objects' is not the same as 'the return of the object' (Foster 2022, p. 150). Returns can come in the form of discovering how objects were made, building better understandings of local histories, relearning traditions, or establishing connections with collecting institutions for wider cultural, social, and economic benefits. Different people will have different interests in different objects.

For many people, the idea of 'return' is the idea of returning to a clean slate. Once objects are returned, the past can be mended and forgotten. Now, we can all get along! However, we know that return does not work in this way. The complexities of the issues remain, and the inequities, misunderstandings, and misrepresentations can linger, but we also need to acknowledge that collecting institutions, source communities, and researchers have begun important reparative work that needs to grow and transform. Increased access to collections and their distribution within source communities – considerably enhanced by digital technologies – is certainly not an endpoint but part of an ongoing process mediated by mutual obligations and new responsibilities. Returning to these collections can pose demanding and difficult questions, reveal painful ruptures, and place significant expectations on already marginalised communities that struggle on multiple fronts.

Finally, in presenting the arguments and case studies in this book, I have tried to remain true to my experiences of working closely with different communities and collecting institutions. Individuals across these contexts have been incredibly generous with me, allowing me to see beyond rhetorical or ideological positioning (in both domains) and grasp something of the way that people and institutions have renegotiated their relationships with these objectified forms and their attendant histories. The politics of repatriation, often presented in morally certain terms and discussed in ways that underestimate the existing tensions, incongruities, and/or contingencies, has simplified our discussions. I hope that this book can contribute to better recognition of the return work that has already been done, the divergent needs and priorities of different communities, and the mixed views on repatriation, which have developed through experience over the years and decades.

## References

Andrews, J. 2017, 'Indigenous Perspectives on Museum Collections', *Artlink*, vol. 37, no. 2, pp. 88–91.

Basu, P. 2021, 'What Should Happen to Colonial Collections That Weren't Looted?' *Apollo*, July, accessed from www.apollo-magazine.com/northcote-thomas-nigeria-sie%E2%80%A6AR38rt5BnLssde8AQ8TTHYUv4Gqz3i1V2JbVVnLhus1DYeEX_TDU6BUjVMo.

Batty, P. 2006, 'White Redemption Rituals: Repatriating Aboriginal Secret-Sacred Objects', in T. Lea, E. Kowal, & G. Cowlishaw (eds), *Moving Anthropology: Critical Indigenous Studies*, Charles Darwin University Press, Darwin, pp. 55–62.

Bennett, T., Cameron, F., Dias, N., Dibley, B., Harrison, R., Jacknis, I. & McCarthy, C. 2017, *Collecting, Ordering, Governing: Anthropology, Museums, and Liberal Government*, Duke University Press, Durham.

Foster, E. 2022, 'Ancestors, Artefacts, Empire: Indigenous Australia in British and Irish Museums by Gaye Sculthorpe, Maria Nugent and Howard Morphy: In Conversation with Eleanor Foster', *ANU Historical Journal*, vol. II, no. 3, pp. 135–150.

Galt-Smith, B. 2001, 'A Certain Trajectory: The Journey of Aboriginal Cultural Material in the Strehlow Collection', in *From Point to Pathway: The Heritage of Routes & Journeys*, Australia International Council on Monuments and Sites, Alice Springs, http://www.aicomos.com/wp-content/uploads/A-certain-trajectory-the-journey-of-Aboriginal-cultural-material-in-the-Strehlow-Collection.pdf.

Gibson, J.M. 2022, '"Factotum and Friend": Anthropologists, Informants and Ethnographic Exchange in Central Australia', *History and Anthropology*, vol. 33, no. 2, pp. 214–242, https://doi.org/10.1080/02757206.2019.1580706.

Glass, A. 2006, 'From Cultural Salvage to Brokerage: The Mythologization of Mungo Martin and the Emergence of Northwest Coast Art', *Museum Anthropology*, vol. 29, no. 1, pp. 20–43, https://doi.org/10.1525/mua.2006.29.1.20.

Glass, A. 2014, 'Indigenous Ontologies, Digital Futures: Plural Provenances and the Kwakwaka'wakw Collection in Berlin and Beyond', in R. Silverman (ed), *Museum as Process: Translating Local and Global Knowledge*, Routledge, London, pp. 19–44.

Glass, A. 2018, 'Drawing on Museums: Early Visual Fieldnotes by Franz Boas and the Indigenous Recuperation of the Archive', *American Anthropologist*, vol. 120, no. 1, pp. 72–88, https://doi.org/10.1111/aman.12975.

Glass, A. 2021, *Writing the Hamat'sa: Ethnography, Colonialism, and the Cannibal Dance*, UBC Press, Vancouver.

Harrison, R., Byrne, S. & Clarke, A. (eds). 2013, *Reassembling the Collection: Ethnographic Museums and Indigenous Agency*, School for Advanced Research Press, Santa Fe.

Hicks, D. 2020, *The Brutish Museum: The Benin Bronzes, Colonial Violence and Cultural Restitution*, Pluto Press, London.

Johnston, I.G., Meara, T., Ley, L., Simpson, C., Lyons, J., Rutherford, R. & Quadri, D. 2021, 'The AIATSIS Return of Cultural Heritage Project: Understanding Aboriginal and Torres Strait Islander Cultural Heritage Material Held Overseas and the Initial Challenges to Repatriating Material to Custodians', *Curator: The Museum Journal*, vol. 64, no. 4, p. 653, https://doi.org/10.1111/cura.12440.

Jonaitis, A. & Glass, A. 2010, *The Totem Pole: An Intercultural History*, University of Washington Press, Seattle, https://trove.nla.gov.au/version/47211620.

Massola, C. Forthcoming, 'Community Collections: Returning to an (Un) Imagined Future', *Museum Anthropology*, vol. 46, no. 1.

Merlan, F. 2005, 'Explorations towards Intercultural Accounts of Socio-Cultural Reproduction and Change', *Oceania*, vol. 75, no. 3, pp. 167–182.

Morphy, H. & McKenzie, R. 2021, *Museums, Societies and the Creation of Value*, Taylor & Francis Group, Milton, UK, accessed from http://ebookcentral.proquest.com/lib/deakin/detail.action?docID=6818323.

Peers, L., Gustafsson Reinius, L. & Shannon, J. 2017, 'Introduction: Repatriation and Ritual, Repatriation as Ritual', *Museum Worlds*, vol. 5, no. 1, pp. 1–8, https://doi.org/10.3167/armw.2017.050102.

Penny, G. 2021, *In Humboldt's Shadow: A Tragic History of German Ethnology*, Princeton University Press, Princeton, NJ.

Peterson, N. 2022, 'Beyond Narratives of Aboriginal Self-Deliverance: Land Rights and Anthropological Visibility in the Australian Public Domain', *Anthropological Forum*, July, accessed from www.tandfonline.com/doi/abs/10.1080/00664677.2022.2084716.

Rowse, T. & Smith, L. 2010, 'The Limits of "Elimination" in the Politics of Population', *Australian Historical Studies*, vol. 41, no. 1, pp. 90–106, https://doi.org/10.1080/10314610903317598.

Turnbull, P. 2017, *Science, Museums and Collecting the Indigenous Dead in Colonial Australia*, Palgrave Studies in Pacific History, Palgrave Macmillan, Cham, Switzerland.

Tweedie, A. 2002, *Drawing Back Culture: The Makah Struggle for Repatriation*. McLellan Endowed Series, University of Washington Press, Seattle, https://ezproxy.deakin.edu.au/login?url=https://search.ebscohost.com/login.aspx?direct=true&db=nlebk&AN=1229082&site=eds-live&scope=site.

Wergin, C. 2021, 'Healing through Heritage? The Repatriation of Human Remains from European Collections as Potential Sites of Reconciliation', *Anthropological Journal of European Cultures*, vol. 30, no. 1, pp. 123–133, https://doi.org/10.3167/ajec.2021.300109.

Wolfe, P. 2006, 'Settler Colonialism and the Elimination of the Native', *Journal of Genocide Research*, vol. 8, no. 4, pp. 387–409, https://doi.org/10.1080/14623520601056240.

# Index

Aboriginal art movement 66–67, 77
Aboriginal cultural heritage, contestation over 74–75, 95
Adnyamathanha people, visions for digital society 1
Ah Kee, Vernon 29–30
Aird, Michael 29
Albrecht, F. W. 43–44
Allen, Lindy 87
Anderson, Chris 67
Angeles, Shaun 12, 39, 41, 42
Anmatyerr Library and Knowledge Centre 36–37
Anmatyerr people/communities 98–99; and Aboriginal art movement 66–67; ceremonial shields 64–65, *65*; connection to place 37; new recordings of songs and ceremonies 63–65; reintegrating of recordings 60–62; repatriation of secret/sacred objects 67, 92–93, 96–97; requests to access Strehlow's recordings 59; responses to digital returns of audio-visual performances 55, 59, 61, 63, 100; rights over intangible cultural property 66; social relationships with collecting institutions 67–68, 73; storage and management of returned recordings 60, 61; storage of new recordings 66; understandings of museums 77; value and treatment of culturally significant objects 77–78
*Anmatyerr shields, songs and ceremonies: a heritage project for community and Nation* 63–64
Ansell, Frank 3
anthropological collections: Arabana people, visions for digital society 1; changes in value and appreciation 16–17; history of collecting 32; recirculation and appropriation of 33
anthropological photography, repurposing 17–19
Arrernte people: awareness of Spencer and Gillen's publications about them 18; ethnographic attention 99; identity 24, 26; and Indigemoji project 19–22; memorialising Irrapmwe 23–26; *mwanty-irreme* 88–89; photographs taken by Spencer and Gillen 17–19, 20–22, *21*, 24, 26; relational ontology 83; and Spencer and Gillen collections website 16; welcome dance 3
Australian Indigenous ancestral remains: Aboriginal communities' responses to return 96; re-burial 82; repatriation 72
Australian Institute of Aboriginal and Torres Strait Islander Studies (AIATSIS) 32; 'Return of Cultural Heritage' programme 75–76

Banks, Joseph 6–7
Barrow Creek Telegraph Station 27
Basu, Paul 7
Berndt, Ronald M. 102
Berndt Museum of Anthropology 31, 102
Bignall, Simone 81
Boas, Franz 8, 16
Bolton, Lissant 17, 61–62
Bray, Tamara 62
Briscoe Mpetyan, Teddy 59
Bruchac, Margaret 11, 12

Cambridge Museum of Archaeology and Anthropology 79
Carty, John 39
ceremonial performances: digital returns of audio-visual performances 54–55;

*see also* Strehlow's audio visual archive
Chakrabarty, Dipesh 80
Clifford, James 80, 81
Cockney Jakkamarra (Warumungu man) 30, 31
collecting: history of 32; new collecting 55–56, 63–65, 66–67, 100
collecting institutions: acknowledgement of diversity of Indigenous epistemologies, values, ontologies, and expectations 82–85; move to paradigms of care 88–89; *see also* museums
collections activism, re-entanglement as form of 7–8
colonialism 82–83
colonial monuments 23
Conference for Museum Anthropologists 74
Cook, James, spears collected by 79
Cook, Rodney 78
'Cook shield' 6–7
Cowle, Charles Ernest 39–40, 41, 42
cultural capital, new collecting as form of 66
cultural endangerment 59, 65, 68, 98–99, 102
cultural heritage sector: Aboriginal peoples as stakeholders or partners 75; impact of postcoloniality, decolonisation and Indigenous methodologies 80
cultural revivals 46, 47–50, 62

Deakin University 102
decolonisation: museum practices 71–72, 81–82, 84–85; overuse of concept 72–73; and transformative collaborations 80–82
Dieri Aboriginal Corporation 47
Dodds, Pat Ansell 23
Dreaming 20, 24, 36, 37, 38, 41, 45
*Dreamings: The Art of Aboriginal Australia* (exhibition) 67
Eagan, Amos 77

Ernest Cowle Collection, project to map object relationships to place 39–43
ethnographic collections: decolonisation 80–82; ethnographic objects as objects of ethnography 11; as intercultural domains 55; re-engagement with 8–10, 101–103; transformative collaborations 71–72, 80–82; *see also* Indigenous collections
ethnography, relational ethnographic methodology 73
excolonialism 81

Field, James 32
Fison, Lorimer 9
Foley, Gary 74
Foster, Warren 48

German museums, destruction of sacred objects during Allied bombings 43
Gillen, Francis 3, 9, 16, 18, 22, 23–24, 26
Gippsland Land and Waters Aboriginal Corporation 47
Glass, Aaron 99
global infosphere, Indigenous responses to 22
Gumula, Joe 4
Gunditjmara people 39
Gweagal people 7
'Gweagal shield' 7

Haddon, Alfred Cort 16
Hagan Mpetyan, Martin 63–64, *65*, 67, 98–99
Haida Emoji Sticker App 20
Haida peoples 7
Hawke, Hazel 67
Hermannsburg Mission 43
Howitt, A. W. 9; notes on 1883 Kuringal ceremony 48–49; transcription and digitisation of his papers 46–47
human remains, repatriation 2
Hunt, George 8

Indigemoji project 19–22
Indigenous Australian musical traditions 54
Indigenous collections: history of production 100–101; intercultural appreciation of 94; production of new knowledge 100–101; re-engagement after return 1–6, 93, 95, 100–101; representation of Indigenous people 95–96; social and cultural labours of re-integrating 98–100; *see also* ethnographic collections

Indigenous epistemologies, values and ontologies, recognition of diversity of 82–85
Indigenous methodologies 80
Indigenous self-determination 75, 84, 94
Ingrey, Ray 79
Inkamala, Mark 39, 41, 42
interculturality 94–96
International Council for Traditional Music 54
Irrapmwe Petharre (aka King Charley; Ntyarlke) 23–25

Kaytetye people 18, 19, 26
Kluge-Ruhe collection 82
Korbula site 58
Krowathunkooloong Keeping Place, Bairnsdale 47
Kuringal ceremony, locating 1883 ceremonial ground 48
Kūrnai community 47, 48
Kwakwaka'wakw community 8, 99

Lamalama people 87
land claims, importance of sacred objects in 44, 50
La Perouse Local Aboriginal Land Council 79
Laramba community: contemporary recording of songs and ceremonies 63–66; response to hearing old recordings 84
Lhere Artepe Aboriginal Corporation 23
Liddle Perrurle, Joel 24–26, *25*, 101
lifeworlds 6
Lock, Annie 37
Lovell, Judy 25
Lynch, Duncan Peltharre 16

Makah communities, Pacific Northwest 98
Marrett, Allan 54
*Mbantua Festival*, Alice Springs 22
McCarthy, Conal 83
McKay Tjungarrayi, Robert 101–102
McNamara, Ronnie 62
Melbourne Museum: arrangement of Indigenous collections 86–87; dramatised film dialogue between Spencer and Irrapmwe 24; failed repatriation of sacred object to Western Arrernte community 44–46; Howitt materials 47; objects produced by Tracker Nat Williams 31; permanent loan of Warumungu objects 33; repatriation project with Strehlow Research Centre 39–40; Spencer and Gillen collections 18; strategy 76; Yolgnu collections 4
Mer Ilpereny 37
Modest, Wayne 82
*Monumental in a small-town way* (exhibition) 24–25, *25*
Morgan, Daniel 48
Morris, Graeme 48
Morton, John 24
Mumbulla, Johnny (aka Jack; King Biamanga) 48–49
Mumbulla, Percy 47, 49
'Mun-ung-unna' (Manangananga) sacred site: cache of sacred boomerangs 43–44; de-sanctification 43
museum catalogues 40–42
Museum of Central Australia, Strehlow Research Centre 39, 40
museum collections: generative qualities 5; Indigenous access to 4, 6–8
museums: Central Australian understandings of 76–79; changes to management of ethnographic museums 72; decolonisation 71–72, 81–82, 84–85; as dialogical space 73, 84; Indigeneity in contemporary management 73–76; interface with Aboriginal communities 10, 12; social relationships with Central Australian communities 67–68, 73; spatial reorganisation of Indigenous collections 85–88; transformative collaborations 81–82
mutual obligation, collecting and 30–32
Myers, Fred 17, 76, 84

National Museum of Australia 39
*Native Tribes of Central Australia* (Spencer & Gillen) 24
new collecting 55–56, 63–65, 66–67, 100
*ngijinkirri* 32, 33
Northern Territory, recognition of Aboriginal land rights 44
Northern Territory Library, *Indigenous Knowledge Centres* program 36–37
*Northern Tribes of Central Australia* (Spencer & Gillen) 26, 27
Nyinkka Nyunyu Art and Cultural Centre, Tennant Creek 33

objects: inherent power of 9; people's return from 102; trajectories of 6–8, 97–98; *see also* secret/sacred objects

Padoon, Paddy 101
Pengart, Don 62
Penny, Glen 94
Phillips, Ruth 12
Pink, Olive Muriel 18
Pintupi peoples 77
Pitt River Museum 7
place: centrality to central Australian Aboriginal ontology 36–38; importance of 38–39; reconnecting with place in country 49–50; relationship between object and 36
Possum Peltharr, Clifford 67
postcolonialism 80
provenance 38–39, 40–41

re-entanglement 7–8, 94–95
relational ethnographic methodology 73
Rengkareka, Titus 43
repatriation: Australian Indigenous ancestral remains 72, 82; challenges of 42, 44–46, 71, 93–94; consultation around 12; conventional notion 8; and decolonisation 71–72; impact on communities 42, 44–46, 93, 99; politics of 104; relationship between place and object 36; rhetoric of 8, 36, 71, 76, 93; secret/sacred objects 67, 92–93, 96–97; as social act 67; theft of repatriated objects 97
reverse fieldwork 11–12
Riley, Rosalie 3
Róheim, Géza 18
Rubuntja, Bob 59

St. Marks Theological College Library 47
salvage anthropology 9, 16, 33
Sculthorpe, Gaye 39, 87
secret/sacred objects: repatriation 67, 92–93, 96–97; theft of repatriated objects 97
settler-colonialism 50, 75, 76, 81
South Australian Museum: digital returns 102; objects produced by Tracker Nat Williams 31; re-burial of Australian Indigenous ancestral remains 82; Spencer and Gillen collections 18; *Statement on the Secret/Sacred Collection* 67; Tindale archive 30
Spencer, Walter Baldwin 3, 9, 16, 22, 23, 24, 26–27, 32, 40
Spencer and Gillen collections 19–22; influence on how Aboriginal peoples were perceived 18; photographs 17–19, 20–22, 24, 26–27, 33; repatriation of Warumungu objects 32–33; website 3, 16, 18, 19, 27–29, 30
Staley, Bevil 27
State Library of Queensland 30
State Library of South Australia 37
State Library of Victoria 47
Strehlow, Carl 58
Strehlow, Theodor George Heinrich 9; background 57; as collector and recordist 56–58
Strehlow Research Centre: digital returns of audio-visual performances 60, 61; establishment and purpose 57; local Indigenous assessment of materials 71; rejected as repository for new recordings 66; spatial reorganisation of collection 83, 85–86
Strehlow's audio visual archive: collaborative returns 58–60; content 56–57, 61; digital return 55, 57, 58
Stuart, John McDouall, statue 23, 24–25

Tamaki Paenga Hira Auckland War Memorial Museum 32–33
Tennant Creek Brio 27
Tennant Creek Telegraph Station 26, 30, 32
Te Papa Museum 83
Thomas, Northcote W. 7
Thomas, Peter 48
Thomas, Ted 47, 48
Thompson, Tommy 18, *19*
Thomson, Donald 87
Tindale, Norman, photographic collection 29–30
Tjampitjinpa, Ronnie 77
Tommy, Michael 54, 55, 64, *65*
transformative collaborations, decolonisation and 80–82
*Transforming Tindale* (exhibition) 29
Turner, Hannah 41
Turner, M.K. 37
Tweedie, Anne 98
*tywerrenge* 50

University of Queensland Anthropology Museum 31
University of Virginia, Kluge-Ruhe collection 82

Wallace, Kathleen 25
Walpiri people 84
Warlayirti Artists 102
Warlukurlangu Artists 102
Warumungu people 17, 26–27, 28–29, *28*, 30–32, 33
Western Arrernte people 43
Wilfred, Graham (Jnr) 22
Williams, Joseph 'Yugi Jungarayi 26, 27–29, *28*, 30–32, 33, 101
Williams, 'Tracker' Nat (aka Warano; Nat Williams Juppurla) 31
Wolfe, Patrick 81
Woods Mpetyan, Big Billy 37
Wurundjeri Council 47

Yerrampe (Arrernte elder) 18
Yolngu people 4
Yuelamu Art Gallery and Museum 67
Yuin community 47, 48–50
Yuelamu community 67

Zulu (Warumungu man) 30

For Product Safety Concerns and Information please contact our EU representative GPSR@taylorandfrancis.com
Taylor & Francis Verlag GmbH, Kaufingerstraße 24, 80331 München, Germany

www.ingramcontent.com/pod-product-compliance
Lightning Source LLC
LaVergne TN
LVHW020643100826
845148LV00012B/2312